PAINTER'S WORKSHOP

RED AND GOLD COLLAGE by Leonard Brooks.

LEONARD BROOKS

PAINTER'S WORKSHOP
A Basic Course in Contemporary Painting and Drawing

VNR VAN NOSTRAND REINHOLD COMPANY
NEW YORK CINCINNATI TORONTO LONDON MELBOURNE

Other books by Leonard Brooks

Painting and Understanding Abstract Art
Oil Painting—Traditional and New
Watercolor—A Challenge

Van Nostrand Reinhold Company Regional Offices:
New York, Cincinnati, Chicago, Millbrae, Dallas

Van Nostrand Reinhold Company Foreign Offices:
London, Toronto, Melbourne

Copyright © 1969 by Reinhold Book Corporation
Library of Congress Catalog Card Number 69-16382

Designed by Jean Callan King. Type set by Lettick Typografic, Inc.
Printed by Halliday Lithograph Corporation. Color printed by The Guinn Company. Bound by William Marley Company.

Published by Van Nostrand Reinhold Company
450 West 33rd Street, New York, N.Y. 10001

Published simultaneously in Canada by
D. Van Nostrand Company (Canada), Ltd.

16 15 14 13 12 11 10 9 8 7 6 5 4 3 2 1

To all past and future members of the *Painter's Workshop* this
book is dedicated, with added thanks to artists, students, and the
many friends who have contributed to the task, especially
to my wife Reva, and Margaret Holton, my editor.

Knowledge evolves, and it is in confronting present problems and
not those of yesterday that the artist has the chance to meet
immutable beauty. He assumes such problems to be the condition
of living in his time and makes them the subject of his work. And
it is through them in the depths of the present, that he must find his
way; beauty is the reward of a personal adventure pursued under
new conditions and not the repetition of what has already been
lived; it is the symbol of a victory over time, not a negation of it.
—Robert Elie

From the foreword of the catalogue for EXPO 67, MAN AND HIS WORLD
International Fine Arts Exhibition, Montreal, Canada.

Color Illustrations

Leonard Brooks	RED AND GOLD	2
	FIRST SNOW	19
	SUNNY MARKET	19
José Luis Cuevas	PROCURESS WITH MEAT	37
Elias Dekoulakos	ANCIENT AND MODERN GREEK	37
Leonard Brooks	NAUTICAL COLLAGES	40
	GRAND CANAL, VENICE	49
	EARLY MORNING, SIENNA	49
Joy Laville	INTERIOR STUDY	52
Mai Onno	ITALIAN VINEYARD	52
Leonard Brooks	MARKING PEN TECHNIQUES	61
	HOMAGE TO R. L.	71
	KNOSSOS	71
	AUTUMNAL	71
Claude Tousignant	TARGET	74
Gordon Smith	SILK SCREEN PRINT	74
Sheldon Cohen	ARRANGEMENT OF ALUMINUM HEXAGONS	74
Claude Breeze	CONTROL CENTER #7	74
Yannis Spyropoulos	INTENTION B	84
Yannis Moralis	THE ULTIMATE SOLUTION	84
Beatrice Mandelman	RED TIME	94
Ghika	ROCKY SHORE	94
Louis Ribak	WHITE CANYON	94
Zdenek Rada	SUN	94
Carlos Mérida	THE ASTROLOGER	95
Nicholas de Staël	HOUSES AT ARGENTEUIL	105
Leonard Brooks	RUSSIAN CIRCUS	105
York Wilson	KABUKI	112
Attilio Carreri	TEMPO DELTA NUMERO 11	112
Rocco Borello	REVERSED STRUCTURAL PAINTINGS	121
Mauro Reggiani	COMPOSIZIONE 15	121
Harold Town	SILENT LIGHT	121
Leonard Brooks	HARBOR AT RHODES	128

CONTENTS

INTRODUCTION   9

1. SOME DRAWING WAYS   11

   What kind of drawing?/Outlines and contours/Elementary perspective/
   Perspective dismissed/Pictorial space/Negative space/ Free form/
   Making a composition/Wind, wall, and sea/Basic drawing/ Sketching/
   What shall I draw?/Figure drawing/Hazards of sketching/
   An ideal "sketchbook box."

2. NAUTICAL ANATOMY   39

3. BASIC TECHNIQUES   45

   Wash drawing/Watercolor/Pastel/Watercolor equipment/
   Texture markings/Some techniques/Cityscapes/The marking pen/
   Basic oil painting technique/Acrylic painting/Collage/Graphics.

4. COLOR   77

   The choice of size.

5. A GROUP OF INTERNATIONAL CONTEMPORARY
   PAINTINGS AND DRAWINGS   83

   Structural space/Six Italian structuralist painters/
   An artist at work/Back to nature/Figurative or abstract?

6. A SCHEDULE FOR *PAINTER'S WORKSHOP*   113

   Checklist of subject to be studied/Basic techniques and materials/
   Twenty-five projects.

7. TODAY AND TOMORROW   145

   Influences and art of our time/Some thoughts on criticism/
   What lies ahead?

BIBLIOGRAPHY   155

INDEX   157

A PIN-UP CHART FOR THE
PAINTER'S WORKSHOP   Insert

Coastal Theme collage by Leonard Brooks. 6 by 5 feet.

NTRODUCTION

How to use this book

This is a book about painting and drawing. Some of it is concerned with the techniques and methods needed to make paintings and drawings; some of it is about the many ways and approaches you can use as a student to find a meaningful direction and purpose to your work. Therefore, at times we will deal with the basic practical matters of materials and their possibilities, and at intervals we will delve into the deeper matters of what and why we are painting — for today, more than ever before in the world of art, we have open to us countless choices of how we wish to express ourselves.

Assuming that you have joined us in our workshop and would like to follow through with us the course suggested here, what are the terms on which we enter? What is to be expected of the instructor as well as of the student? Let us clarify this at the outset.

When this book was first started it was in the form of a personal note-book in which, from time to time, the author jotted down notes he felt would be of value to his students in the studio workshops he has held in various universities, art schools, and summer seminars, where groups of enthusiasts, young and old, beginners and more experienced students, came together for intensive, short courses in contemporary painting and drawing. The informal, intimate character of these courses was ideal for an interchange of ideas and afforded, as well, a valuable proving ground in which many of the problems of the painter today were explored and studied. For the instructor it was always a warming experience to feel and see these groups of disparate individuals working independently yet mutually concerned in solving the many problems of each other's creative efforts.

In such an atmosphere one soon finds out what a variety of teaching is open to the instructor. Shall he concentrate on drawing? How much time should be given to working in color, or in black and white? How soon will the student find real understanding and pleasure in transposing objectivity into abstraction — how soon is he ready to throw aside many of the basic fundamentals, which for years were considered essential to working with any kind of skill and authority? How much can be taught, and how much should be left to the individual to struggle with and find for himself? What does "background" consist of, and is it even necessary to have one to produce the kind of painting approved and applauded today as being "non-art," "non-painterly," but which seems to be only a negation of all the forms and ways we have known in the past?

Some of these questions are discussed herein, as they must be in any Painter's Workshop that professes to be concerned with contemporary painting and with the changes that have swept and are sweeping the world of art today.

This, then, primarily, we ask of the instructor: that he be a working and experienced artist, very much alive to what is happening now, as well as to what has happened in the past. We must ask of him that he embrace a vision of drawing and painting that reaches far beyond the personal manner he has chosen for his own work. There is nothing so discouraging as the "art class" that ends its findings with nothing more than a superficial imitation of the teacher's own solutions and style.

Secondly, and this is of utmost importance, a painter of integrity should be able to impart to his students the love for his profession that he himself has known; love and a respect for a profession that has had, these last few years, a difficult and disquieting period in which lack of criteria — and worse — a rampant commercialism — has made many a young painter cynical and discouraged.

So much for the instructor. What must we ask of the student?

The first requirements are, of course, enthusiasm and keen interest in our subject. With these precious ingredients we can begin with a minimum of training and experience. Without them, we are lost before we even start, and we might just as well put this book away, take our name off the list for studio space, and go play golf or practice on the piano, using our energies and leisure time at something nearer to our hearts than drawing or painting. If we *are* really interested and deeply desire to paint, much of our battle is won. If we have already tested ourselves in the field of plastic arts and know how the joys and tribulations, the chores and disappointments, of painting and drawing are rewarded only in ratio to the amount of vigorous effort we put into the matter, we are more than ready to accept the challenges and suggested projects ahead of us.

Some skill and ability on the reader's part is assumed. Very few of us have not been exposed to some kind of instruction in drawing and use of paint during our lifetimes, but even this is not of the utmost importance. I have often had completely inexperienced students and amateurs in my classes who have been able, with hard work and sensitivity, to produce surprisingly interesting and imaginative results, stamped with originality and vitality that outshone many a so-called "semi-professional." The latter, bogged down in his own tired facility and repetitious "successes," is the inevitable member in our midst who knows all the answers, has closed his mind to new ideas, and has solved his problems and everyone else's before he appears on the scene. An air of smouldering resentment and prejudice hangs like a rancid perfume about him, which somehow even manages to mix itself, acidly, into the colored pigments on his canvas.

Enthusiasm, then, and an open mind are necessary requisites. You must have patience to go along with ideas and methods that perhaps you have already examined closely, and with new ideas that may appear difficult to you. *Painter's Workshop* gives you a set plan of action, augmented by a removable chart of scheduled work designed to be hung above your drawing board or painting easel. One subject at a time, one element of all those complicated pieces we have had only a little space to touch upon in this book, should be studied as we shape up our larger purpose of giving ourselves a progressive rounded-out course of study in some of the basic techniques every art student should have at his command.

There are some teachable things we can pass along and we shall try to do so. We want you to see how much a painting is a matter of emotion, of intellectual controls, of rejections and adjustments within the particular work and its form, be it abstract or figurative. We want you to start to feel and work with sensitivity and intelligence.

It would be easy to say that I can take you by the hand, step by step, making everything rational and clear. I could tell you, as some instructors will, that you should shun all teachers and books and keep your soul flowing out on paper and canvas, or that you should study hard for twenty years at art school and then emerge triumphantly. Neither of these ways will work. Most serious art students begin their painting lives somewhere between these two — a compromise. They follow along the strong current of the best they can find in the art world of their time, unashamedly influenced by the work about them. Then they grow, see, and feel something new within themselves and fling loose, taking with them what they need for their individual ways. This is when artistic maturity begins. We look at a man's work and begin to see something more in it than a display of skills or imitation of work accomplished by others. That is when an art student or amateur begins to be — an artist.

1. SOME DRAWING WAYS

What kind of drawing?, 12

Outlines and contours, 14

Elementary perspective, 15

Perspective dismissed, 20

Pictorial space, 22

Negative space, 24

Free forms, 25

Making a composition, 26

Wind, wall, and sea—Hydra, 28

Basic drawing, 31

Sketching, 31

What shall I draw?, 32

Figure drawing, 33

Hazards of sketching, 36

An ideal "sketchbook box," 38

SOME DRAWING WAYS

What kind of drawing?

What kind of drawing do you want to do and what do you need to know about it? Curiously, this does not often occur to the student until someone asks him this obvious question. The language of drawing is a complex one, involving any subject in various media, and ranges from hum-drum mechanical rendering to the inspired skills of the great masters. In painting pictures you do not have to learn to draw like an architect and, judging by most architectural drawings I have seen, it would be fatal to learn how. Some of the knowledges an architect must have can prove useful to you, however, such as an understanding of elementary perspective and some forms of "rendering," but most architectural drawing methods have little to do with the real problem of drawing and painting today.

The marks and signs made by a genuine artist of experience are far different from the first gropings and scrawls of a child or scribbles by an unskilled hand, but these differences are not always apparent. The reasons why they are *not* like the work of a child or a beginner are not always easily explained, any more than we can explain the difference between the tone and quality of a genius with the violin and an ordinary, well trained, run-of-the-mill musician. They use the same fingers, the same strings, the same notes, but what comes out of these techniques is far from being the same result. Sensitivity, the instinctive capacity that makes a fine drawing, is just not explainable, though we may do our best to analyze and dissect the work of art in a thousand ways. We may discover some of the reasons *why* it works, but these reasonings will not suddenly produce another masterpiece.

Drawing for today's art often requires different skills and attitudes than those used in earlier centuries. We seldom need the highly-trained ability assumed to be part of every art student's or artist's equipment even just a few years ago. The specialized eye of the portrait painter who has only trained his hand and eye to catch a perfect likeness in charcoal or pencil finds little occupation today. When commissioned to do portraits, the demand for his work will depend upon his expressive and personal vision and interpretation, rather than the accurate presentation or literal descriptive copying of his model.

Today, a young painter can build his entire reputation and career without being able to "draw" in the accepted sense of the word. Blown-up photographs, silk-screened prints from newspaper clippings, rubbings, and other means of reproduction are acceptable. As a geometric structuralist, a painter needs only to know how to use ruler, compass, and masking tape; the "optical" artist shuns the vagaries of a loose and personal line, the accidental qualities of nervous, free outlines and sketchy qualities, and strives only for the disciplined mechanical surface to make his communication clear and defined. Drawing in this form is not a problem to even the beginning student, and the rejection of drawing in the classic sense by many students who work in the purity of geometric idioms is understandable. In fact, it is quite conceivable that drawing in the "Old Master" sense, as we have known it, will eventually disappear and become another of the lost arts or skills, much as many of the incredibly skillful and refined crafts of early wood-engravers and etchers have been lost, or at least changed to suit the needs of today's graphic expression.

Today, drawing in traditional ways is often purposely rejected, the "non-art," "unpainterly" quality insisted upon, the stamp of the individual carefully omitted, or, when it does intrude, stamped out or erased as ruthlessly as once the artist strove to encourage and nurture his personal and unique expression, at all costs.

This elusive search for sparsity — this destroying of all values and aesthetic criteria we have cherished in the past — is, for our changed world, often a healthy and needed cleansing of cluttered worn-out ways. It can also be a destructive influence that throws the baby out with the bath water and leaves only vacuity and a hollow sense of futility. It may leave in its wake cheap easy imitations instead of an honest and painful re-examination of our basic values and work of lasting value.

What then the need for training the eye and hand to measure out proportion, to render with some degree of accuracy the lines and forms of face, figure, or landscape, or to master the flow of brush-stroke and paint? I suppose, truthfully, the answer is "none" if you are painting in a manner that needs nothing more than two or three flat areas of paint, or perhaps a stripe or two down the center. A good yardstick and the ability to stick down tape or peel it off are the only essential crafts you will require. Such traditional matters as we will be studying will not be of much value to you, either, if you are working with lights and sound, plastic sheeting to wrap objects or whole rooms in, assembling old chairs and motorcycle engines in boxes, or making plexi-glass boxes, or painting spare white or black canvases. Such a repudiation of drawing and painting as we have thought of it for centuries is a legitimate attitude for many young artists. The tyranny of the paintbrush and its rejection from such contemporary studios is understandable.

Yet there are many of us who still love to "draw," not necessarily in a representational or "realist" style, but in a manner that exploits all the wonderful and exciting qualities inherent in many time-honored media — wash-drawing, watercolor, pen and ink, pencil, and charcoal — all the tools of the artist and craftsman who finds pleasure in their expressive and many-varied voices. That these voices have other songs to sing and new ways of singing for today is as it should be; that other voices are stilled or go unheard is a pertinent and revealing commentary on our times.

With the belief that most serious artists and students feel that they need some drawing skill, no matter in which style or direction their final work may end, I am including in this course technical material and information I think will be helpful. This is not to insist that our students must go through endless courses, studying anatomy, perspective, and design. It *does* require that you absorb some of the knowledges developed and used by thousands of fine creative painters who, in their research and work, have stored valuable treasures for us in our pursuit of art forms for our times.

OUTLINES AND CONTOURS

Such "inventorial" drawings will develop a decorative and sensitive line. No "blocking out" of shapes first, and no fast sketchy line. Begin somewhere on the page and start drawing — directly, slowly, and with even controlled line. Let the eye travel slowly over the objects to be drawn, moving the pen on the paper in the same time sequence. Keep away from dark accents and shadow indications; use pure even line only. Such cataloguing of fact is another way of training your eye for the recording of more profound seeing, later.

ELEMENTARY PERSPECTIVE

Knowing how to sketch in perspective can contribute to expanding your creative expression, in spite of what some art teachers may say to the contrary. An understanding of the elementary laws of perspective illusion can be easily acquired in a short period of study, and then be absorbed or discarded at will, its lesson tucked away when working in your own individual freer manner. Knowing when *not* to use perspective or when to use whatever part you wish to use is a far different thing than rejecting its laws because you know nothing about them. I have seen too many trite and distressing amateur and student works where the lack of knowledge of a few simple rules reveals itself in obvious fashion — drawings lacking constructive sense, no control of pictorial space, the awkward and uncontrolled handling of recession and pictorial depth. A few sessions with the problems of perspective and the study of its use or its discard and rejection in their work would have been valuable to them, no matter in what style they worked.

There are too many good books available on perspective to try to develop the subject in detail in this short space. It is sufficient for our purpose to review the use of one-point and two-point "vanishing" points — imaginary dots on the horizon line, or eye level, *where all parallel lines turned at an angle to our picture-plane will appear to meet.*

Imagining our picture plane as a sheet of glass in front of us, a window through which we look, will help us to find the angle at which lines appear to recede up or down to the horizon line. If we climb up, the horizon line moves up with our eyes. The Guardi drawing illustrates a one vanishing point drawing, as does the sketch made aboard a ship (page 18) to illustrate how all the lines run to a single point on the level with the viewer's eye — the point of vision on the horizon.

Two-point perspective has two sets of receding lines. A book, when parallel to our window surface, has its two sides (parallel lines) receding to *one* vanishing point. Turn it at an angle to the "window" (or picture plane) and it has *two sets* of vanishing points on the eye level (or horizon line). Every time we change the angle of the book from parallel to the picture plane (our window surface) we find that the vanishing points move along the horizon line. Each angle has its own vanishing point. Six books with six different angles will produce for us twelve vanishing points on the

TEATRO LA FENICE by Francesco Guardi (1712-1793). Pen and wash. (Courtesy The Metropolitan Museum of Art, Rogers Fund, 1937.)

LOGGIA OF A PALACE by Francesco Guardi (1712-1793). Pen and wash. (Courtesy The Metropolitan Museum of Art, Rogers Fund, 1937.)

15

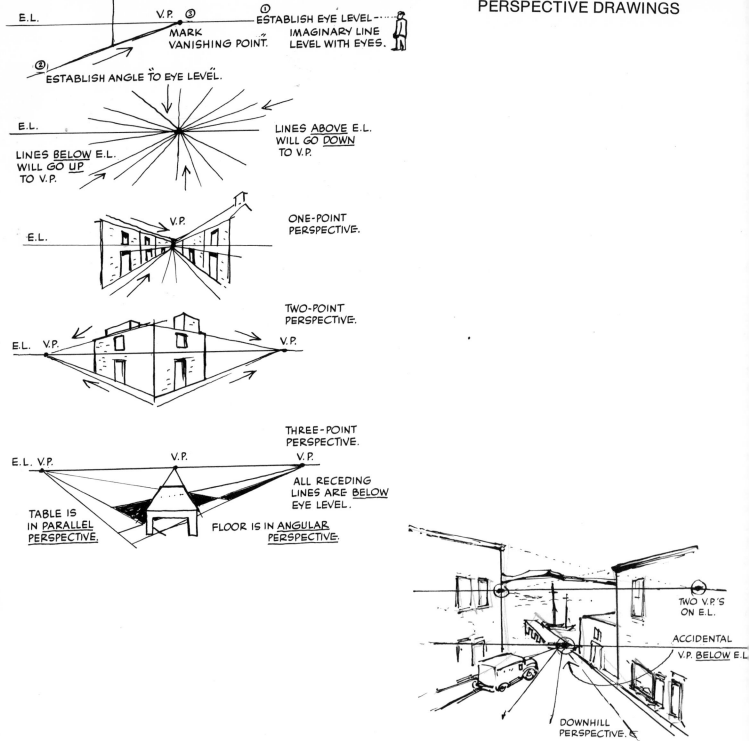

E.L.   V.P. ③   ① ESTABLISH EYE LEVEL —
MARK VANISHING POINT.   IMAGINARY LINE LEVEL WITH EYES.

② ESTABLISH ANGLE TO EYE LEVEL.

E.L.

LINES BELOW E.L. WILL GO UP TO V.P.

LINES ABOVE E.L. WILL GO DOWN TO V.P.

E.L.   V.P.   ONE-POINT PERSPECTIVE.

TWO-POINT PERSPECTIVE.

E.L.   V.P.   V.P.

THREE-POINT PERSPECTIVE.

E.L. V.P.   V.P.   V.P.

ALL RECEDING LINES ARE BELOW EYE LEVEL.

TABLE IS IN PARALLEL PERSPECTIVE.

FLOOR IS IN ANGULAR PERSPECTIVE.

TWO V.P.'S ON E.L.

ACCIDENTAL V.P. BELOW E.L.

DOWNHILL PERSPECTIVE.

V.P. 1   V.P. 2   E.L.   V.P. 3

EVERY CHANGE OF ANGLE HAS ITS V.P. ON E.L.

horizon line. This rule applies to houses, streets, furniture, and all architectural solids. We assume, of course, that all of these objects are on a horizontal plane, not on tilted planes.

Add to this that all lines above the horizon line at an angle to the picture plane go *down* to the vanishing point, and all those below our horizon line, or eye level, go *up* to meet the horizon line.

Inclined planes will recede to an accidental vanishing point which is *not* to be found on the eye level. Slanting roofs and book covers, up-and-down-hill lines — all of these parallel lines do not recede to a point *on* the eye level but to one *above* or *below* the eye level.

In most perspective grids, on which you will visualize your subjects, the vanishing points will be found *outside* your paper edges. Most beginners do not judge the angle approaching the horizon correctly but have a tendency to make it too wide or too acute. This gives their drawings a "tipped up" feeling of recession, which can be unpleasant unless done for compositional purposes and with reason. Cézanne and Braque used this device to flatten out the pictorial space, tilting tables up to the picture plane and changing the foreshortening of the table.

Apart from the use of perspective to represent reality, its practice can, if we use it for such a purpose, help us to define and sense solids and three-dimensional form in our mind's eye and to project these without trouble when we need to on our paper or canvas. After some practice with imagining shapes and forms of actual objects — can you draw a cube, a cone, and a cylinder in perspective? — we can juggle them, draw them in any position we wish or fuse them in complex relationships on the flat surface of our paper. We can begin to control *pictorial space*. Then we are free to forget the rules of perspective and impose form as we wish on our own composition according to our dictates. We can produce illusion of space, of going *back* into the picture plane, or we can flatten it out at will. We can negate or emphasize depth, creating movement back and forth into pictorial space as well as producing lines that stress the flatness and two-dimensionality of our picture surface. This is the simple explanation of much that may seem mysterious when you read involved scholarly treatises about the Cézanne theory or other space concepts of composing, or when you find yourself bewildered by such things as negative space, the "integrity" of the picture plane, deep pictorial recession, tensions, static and dynamic fields, and so on.

The illustrations on page 23 should make evident a few of the visual possibilities you can use in your study

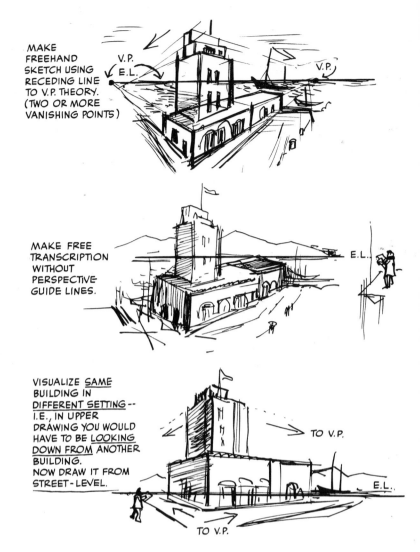

MAKE FREEHAND SKETCH USING RECEDING LINE TO V.P. THEORY. (TWO OR MORE VANISHING POINTS)

MAKE FREE TRANSCRIPTION WITHOUT PERSPECTIVE GUIDE LINES.

VISUALIZE SAME BUILDING IN DIFFERENT SETTING -- I.E., IN UPPER DRAWING YOU WOULD HAVE TO BE LOOKING DOWN FROM ANOTHER BUILDING. NOW DRAW IT FROM STREET-LEVEL.

of lines and space, as well as what happens when we use accents and mass in combination. Overlappings, "fracturing" planes of objects seen from two or three viewpoints and then presented in one drawing on one picture plane can be seen in any book on the experiments of the Cubists.

These changes are accepted and taken for granted in the contemporary usage and technique of the artist. New teachings have in turn been absorbed, rejected, and other new findings added to the visual languages of our ever-changing world of art. Some will be dealt with in a later session. Meanwhile, let us make a few trial drawings of the kind we have discussed in this brief study of perspective thinking.

Understanding the recession of clouds is helped by perspective seeing.

Two freehand wash perspective sketches made on the spot from subjects that required perspective thinking. Up-hill street uses an eye-level placed well down *below* the center of the page. The deck view of a ship places the eye-level well *up* on the upper third of the drawing.

FIRST SNOW by Leonard Brooks. Oil on canvas.

SUNNY MARKET by Leonard Brooks, Oil on canvas.

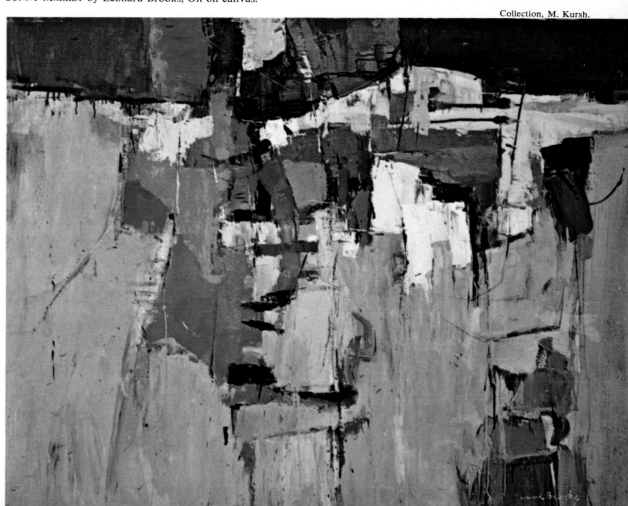

PERSPECTIVE DISMISSED

Some of the fascination we find in old prints and drawings comes from the rejection or non-use of the perspective rules we have just considered. The naïve and primitive projection of pictorial space in ancient wood blocks and in illustrations found in illuminated manuscripts obtain much of their impact and decorative attraction from this very lack.

Reproduced on page 21 are drawings I copied from an illustrated history of churches and retreats in a Grecian monastery. These drawings were not done by sophisticated artists; they were recorded by monks and artisans in their mountain homes, where they worked and lived.

It is interesting to compare these drawings with later and more popular kinds made by Western artists who overwhelmed Europe with detailed landscape sketches, later engraved and reproduced in the many travel books published at the time. How dull many of these look in comparison with the early naïve drawings, although factually more accurate and visually correct. They so much lack the intimate feeling of the places recorded.

We know how the monks were influenced by Byzantine tradition, isolated as they were and subject to their inheritance of icons, ancient frescoes, and illuminated vellum volumes in their chapel libraries. The twelfth and thirteenth centuries were still alive to them and the forms beloved by Giotto and other great painters had been absorbed and emulated in patient repetition for centuries, becoming part of the accepted convention for the artist-monks, as natural to them as eating one meal a day or being hauled in sacks up almost inaccessible mountain crags.

We note the tipping up of planes, the placing of objects higher and above other objects to suggest distance and space. Observe the slanting parallel lines of the side of the church and how these do not appear to meet as they get further away. This isometric projection is similar to the kind of drawing we often do for the carpenter to use when making a table or box. It is a plan, rather than a visual perspective convention.

If we stood on the same spot as the sketching monk did we would not see his vista in the manner he has drawn it. He has drawn what he *knows* is there as much or more than what he actually sees. Yet how it comes alive for us — the tower, the walls, and roofs.

The *idea* of the place is put down for us as each fact is catalogued and noted. The very limitations of his form of spatial projection has brought the reality of the place into vivid depiction, without the use of scientific perspective theory.

But merely making pictures *without* perspective is only the beginning. When we study and analyze Cubist paintings of our century we find how they fused traditional limitations with the new knowledges at the command. We see them experimenting with two or more viewpoints in one picture plane, we see reverse perspective, fracturing of planes, and many other devices to make more "real" and more alive their ideas and interpretations of objectivity. We see them using the Oriental, Byzantine, and other great periods of art in new and vital ways.

Note tipping of planes and the use of isometric perspective in the table, cradle, and doorway in this Byzantine icon, which is reminiscent in parts of a Braque still-life painting, in its conception

1790

2

A drawing that obtains much of its appeal from a naïve but authentic stylization based on the Byzantine sense of spatial projection.

A street in a village disregards size diminution, receding parallel lines, and perspective. The horse and the figure stand in their own space, positioned and related to the houses without regard to proportion and size, which would be evident if the perspective grid were used. The water tank holds fish that would spill out with the water at the angle shown, yet the *idea* of the place is made very real to us, the pictorial "plan" is clear.

Make a drawing trying to imagine yourself on the spot somewhere near the fish tank. What you would *see* probably would be something like the sketch we show here. The buildings have been compressed, the right-angles foreshortened, the figures made smaller in the distance. More correct perhaps, but something has been lost in this perspective projection of the spatial reality of the scene.

3

21

PICTORIAL SPACE

The dividing of space in our picture is the first act of our composing problem. We may do it with lines, symmetrical measure, uneven spaces; it may be balanced, off-balance, static, dynamic. We may make our divisions instinctively, seeking variety, or in geometric relationships of proportion and measure, or by mechanical methods, such as the "Golden Cut" and Dynamic Symmetry. The boundaries, the format of our picture, affect and change the spaces, dots, forms, and shapes contained in the chosen shape we use for our composition. An isolated diagonal line assumes many different visual identities according to its placing in the outlines of a square or rectangle as well as in its association with its neighboring shapes. Its energy and thrust may be blocked, counteracted, crossed with other lines. The artist can direct his visual forces to creating movement — that is, to guide the eye across the picture surface from accent to accent — form to form. He may add tensions, suggest emotions with rhythmic beat and time sequence, create empty pauses as well as counterpoint of light and dark intervals. He is concerned with the shapes of the object itself — the positive volumes — as well as the *negative* space, which is the physical emptiness of space surrounding the object, forming a background on the flat pictureplane.

The movement *back into pictorial space* must be considered, for there are sensations of movement into shallow and deep space when we survey the flat surface of the picture, although this is an illusion, as, of course, there is no actual depth. We can control this sensation of pictorial depth by limiting the perception of depth, much as we can control the eye on its perusal of the flat horizontal and vertical movement of the picture surface. We have shown some of these controlled depth sensations and how we may achieve them by overlapping planes, flattening pictorial space, and by stressing horizontal and vertical lines and planes, controlling perspective and deep space. The artist uses all of these compositional devices, studies the energies and related forces of his lines and forms and marshals them to his desired statement by using the dynamics of visual form. He sensitizes himself to feel the sensuous power of contrasting curved forms, the stern and dignified rigidity of a line of verticals, the passive feeling of horizontal lines suggestive of rest and calm, the visual, potent energy in a dot or series of dots when placed against the contrasting emptiness of the

white surface on which he paints. He takes the reality of the object and shakes it for what it is worth, finding its pictorial essence and only what is required for his painting. He detaches, purifies, exaggerates, underplays, breaks and remakes. Selection, rejection, the harnessing of spatial illusion and projection of imaginative and personal images, the putting-in, the enlarging, the diminishing, the enriching, or simplifying — all of these form a different part of the difficult language of composing.

Composition is not a system, a recipe, a series of rules and tricks, which, once learned, make composition a facile task. Each picture is a new problem, a new adventure in creating a fresh visual excitement and experience. "A painting well-composed is half-done," said Bonnard. Knowing some workable rules that have helped in other experimental drawings can be useful to you, but don't consider them infallible or always applicable to your own compositional solutions. Carefully studying successful paintings and then asking yourself *why* they work can be invaluable. Trying some of the exercises suggested here will help.

. Using pen and ink, draw directly and without concern for perspective rules a series of solids, constructing these from your imagination in any relationship you wish.

. Draw a series of horizontal planes and platforms projecting into pictorial space. Do not worry about receding lines or vanishing points. Each solid must explain itself, i.e., you should be able to construct an actual dimensional object easily from your descriptive drawing.

. Invent tubular and cylindrical objects in such a manner that the forms could be modelled in clay from your drawing. These will help you to develop your sense of form and its projection and to understand spatial relationships.

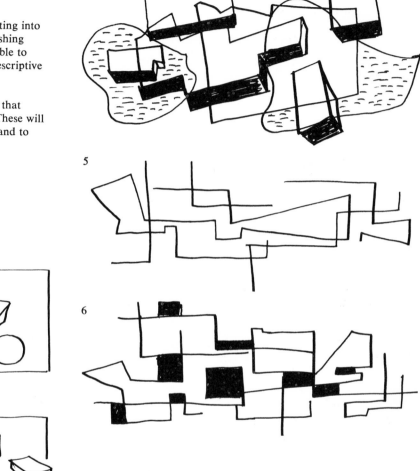

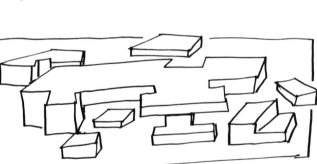

4. Projection of three-dimensional forms plus shapes and areas of a negative or flat kind will set up visual movements of varied depths in pictorial space. Overlappings or transparent "see through" will bring the eye to bear sorting out movement in and behind — shifting space in pictorial depth.

5. Using outlines only, observe how some lines will provoke space sensation, one line making a plane that appears to be in front of or behind another.

6. The addition of black accent to pure line increases the suggestion of space and defines it more clearly. Dominant blacks come forward in their spatial position. Such simple design experiments are part of the dynamics of visual form that the Cubists and the later geometric abstractionists made to clarify and widen our visual language.

NEGATIVE SPACE

The shapes created in and about positive forms. The interlocking of flat surfaces on the picture plane must be considered by the artist in making his composition on the flat surface of his picture. The flattening of planes and the dismissal of the perspective illusion is a common technique of contemporary painting. Shown here are a number of examples in which negative space and the overall flatness of surface is stressed. The collage still life shows this approach in its strongly designed emphasis and "fracturing" of planes.

1

2

3

4

FREE FORM

The highly-charged free swing of a brush can invent rhythmic and organic forms that use the dynamics of form without reference to objectivity or actual subjects. These rapid "action" expressions will often contain in themselves a balance, variety, and movement that please us with their spontaneous automatism. The white areas — negative space — are carefully considered in these free forms.

1. A speedball pen was used to make the first drawing.

2. The curve was developed with rapid calligraphy, much like the writing technique of Chinese brushed letters, freely and fluidly drawn.

3. The free scrawl is carefully redrawn, using the lines and shapes of Figure 1. as a basis for a much more formal rendering.

4. A section of the drawing is selected and drawn in reverse, white on black. In such an exercise you will enjoy seeing your first original theme emerging in new and exciting form..

Making a composition

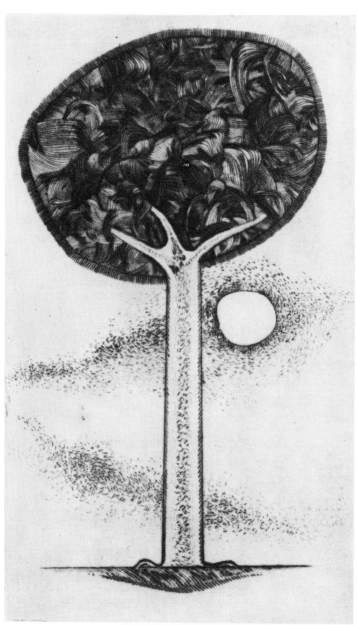

Etching by Ivan Dobroruka.

We have said that to compose is to combine the visual elements of line, tonal textures, pictorial space, or black and white qualities and color into a complete and satisfactory whole. Sometimes we call it designing, organizing, orchestrating. Expressive composing demands that each part, each detail, must contribute to the overall and complete statement and must contain within itself the feeling of organic growth, each part related and organized to express the idea and inner experience of the artist. Its technique is restricted by the flat surface or picture plane and imaginary depth or pictorial space can be controlled, emphasized, or eliminated at will by the artist. Most contemporary artists have found new ways of expressing spatial depth, other ways than the traditional perspective we discussed before.

Styles and "isms" come and go in cycles but underlying these changing modes of expression is the inner necessity for man to express himself and to communicate his feelings. As an artist he may do this through any of the many ways open to him, using the techniques of picture making in traditional or new ways. He is forever seeking new means, exploring beyond the limitations of accepted and well-worn solutions of the creative process. The immense variety of possible manners or styles of working open to him today are greater than ever before in history, the range of possible directions he may go ever expanding as new knowledges and technological advances are made. New forms, new feelings, new experiences will constantly demand new expression. The reactions of today's artist are of necessity different; the material and subjects with which he works reflect changed attitudes and the responses of man to his new environment.

The putting together of a composition, the search for this perfect harmony and completeness of a perfected expression, is one of the most mysterious functions of the artist. We *know* when it is right; it *does* fulfill all its promise, moving us, delighting us, communicating and arousing us as a great work of art should. *Why* it does so, what inexplicable force has directed the artist's brush, just why it moves us, is most often a baffling and unanswerable question. We may analyze, dissect, verbalize; it may help us to understand, but the secret too often reaches beyond our reasonings and probing. We know how Mozart wrote down his music, we know what his counterpoint and style consist of, we may even do a good job of imitating it — but no one can tell us how or from where came the inspiration for his divine melodies and glorious music.

Composition then, must serve us to express our ideas. We must learn its limitations, and its possibilities, knowing that when we are all through our studies we have only touched the fringe of the real problem. All the rules, analyses, and explanations in the world will not help us make a fine composition if we have not at the same time increased our sensitivity, sharpened our feelings, understood that principles of design and composition are only straws in the wind to aid us in increasing our inventive and expressive powers. The wind itself blows hard and violently, and we must throw ourselves figuratively in its buffeting and frigid path — if we are fortunate enough to have it blow in our direction. Then, perhaps, we may make order out of chaos, search for our own solutions and answers to produce something that is not a mere echo of the work of others who have already braved the stormy force of that true creative endeavour that overrides rules and academic regulations of how we supposedly can make a composition that is a work of art.

Accepted and useful reasonings about composing may help you. Some of them are outlined here. Study some of the various compositions illustrated in this book. They have been chosen from works by artists in many fields of endeavour in many parts of the world. Abstract, realistic, semi-abstract. Why do they "work"? What is the idea behind the design, the marks, colors, textures? Do they please or repel us? How and why have certain artists stripped away all but sheer structure, leaving only the geometric forms as an element of feeling? Do we prefer complex design and enrichments, or the austere structural qualities behind the geometry? Do we like our composition baldly revealed, stripped of its brush-marking, textures, and interpretative drawing? Do we prefer tidy cleaned-up patterning and stark formation to the intricate new Baroque, art-nouveau, whirling scrolls, and dream-like fantasy of line and form? Do we want our picture to leave us shocked with impact, or do we prefer to be gently led into the devious and concealed visual pleasures awaiting a sophisticated well-trained eye?

With time, we would delve into the past, seek our early and primitive composing, trace the changes in the accepted styles and expressive modes from the

"grand" style of the Baroque, the Renaissance, the classical French and Italian works. We would follow through the revolutionary times of the Fauves, of the Expressionists, and put down, as we did in the book *Understanding and Painting Abstract Art* (Reinhold), the churning battles of the last seventy-five years of experimental and abstract painting, which led to the non-figurative abstraction we use today. Most of this study research you must do for yourself, a task made easier these days, in libraries containing scholarly surveys of art movements and the times that brought them into being.

Steps in developing a composition from the first broad divisions of spacing of format to the textured and enriched design.

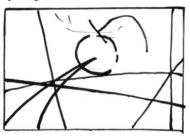

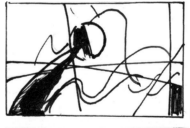

WIND, WALL, AND SEA—HYDRA

The subject lay outside my studio in Hydra, Greece, and each morning I arose to look out of the window at the clear Aegean light filtering over the harmony of brown, ochre, and white walls interlocked in intricate pattern aslant a rocky hillside.

One day the wind joined forces with the sea, churning up a dancing wild body of foam-capped water. The air vibrated with the howling of a northern gale and shook the two-hundred-year-old sea-captain's house on its eagle-nest perch, in which was my studio.

Wind, wall, and sea. The idea and objects fused into a concept that could be painted. The studies I had done earlier, some ink drawings, watercolors, and acrylics, must now be put to good use; a totality of mood and feeling be made from the many impressions I had noted. Facts would now be changed, the vista widened. All must add up to a strong synthesis with a dominent mood and theme. The idea must be clearly presented and all externals thrust aside.

Some of the changes made may be seen by comparing the illustrations. Space has been altered, the flat surface emphasized. Each area demands its answering space in an organic whole. Lights, darks, colors, and forms must move in time sequence across and through the painting. The raw material must be forced to the will of our idea and transfigured. Textures are created, lines and shapes integrated, and the underlying abstract structure concealed — this is the foundation on which the design hangs, which must, in finality, deliver the message of the painting.

1. Photograph of the subject.

2. Tonal drawing.

3. Vertical version.

4. Abstract of the subject.

5. WIND, WALL, AND SEA — HYDRA, finished painting done in acrylics.

ROOFTOPS AND ACROPOLIS, bamboo pen drawing by Leonard Brooks. This large full-page drawing was made as the final drawing of a series. In it, the many facts of steep walls, houses, and streets of the ancient *Plaka* are simplified. The glow of morning light is suggested by the use of white paper and some lightly-toned shadow forms. Details are suppressed in favor of suggestion and vignetted pattern. The eye takes and uses only the lines and forms it wants to use. Knowing when to stop with this kind of drawing is important.

Below are two smaller versions of the same subject, one in line and one with added washes, made on the same morning, before the larger page version above was drawn.

Basic drawing

SKETCHING

MOTHER AND CHILD by Robert Maxwell.
Wash drawing.

"To be able to seize upon the essential lines and shapes of a subject and to put these down simply and clearly, capturing the mood and feeling by skillful use of whatever medium is being employed, is a pleasure reserved for the hardy breed of artists known as sketchers." They are those who, in the great tradition of Rembrandt, Turner, and Edward Lear, love to fill notebooks with recordings of what they see and feel about the world around them. All is grist for their mill, and they will be found sketching in crowded buses and trains, on city streets, in buildings, while climbing steep mountains, haunting the market-places and harbors of the world, or while just wandering about a garden, noting the forms of insects, bees, and butter-lies, or the beauty revealed in the curl of a rose petal or cabbage leaf.

That they are a hardy lot is not to be denied. Have you seen one of their breed drawing in the midst of a band of curious onlookers who seem to find it needful to stand directly in front of the subject the sketcher is stalking? Have you watched them fighting flies, noise, and smells in crowded streets and markets, or seen them shivering at the entrance of a snow-covered alleyway noting down a chilly subject? Or seen them carting their materials over miles of summer roadways or in hot ghetto streets, when the people, light, and air seem just right for long hours of work, sitting wherever there is a convenient spot, oblivious of all else but the subject?

A mad lot indeed, but all of them, from the beginner to the old professional, are tinged with an overpowering interest and love for this world and its people, and the wonderous things in it to be seen and depicted. Whether their specialty is drawing figures or animals, cityscape or countryside, or all of them, they need defer to no one in the gladness and joy they experience when everything goes right and a morning's hard work is rewarded with a few more pages filled in their sketchbooks, trophies of a successful and exciting hunt.

The other day I was returning from Mexico City on the bus. Behind me sat three art students who, confident that none of the other passengers understood English, confided to each other their young woes and trials at art school. Although I was trying to rest, I sat up in my seat with a start when I heard one weary young voice say, ". . . I just don't like to draw, it's a bore, man. The teacher told us it wasn't necessary anyway."

Came another more sophisticated voice, "You're right, man. If you are drawing on a higher level, you don't need basic training."

I quote these words literally, for I took out my notebook and jotted down exactly what I had just heard, to make sure later, that I had not invented them.

Now I think I know what that second voice meant, for I have been trying for a number of years to discover and to progress to this mysterious "higher level," which seems to haunt so many of us. I have written a good many words and talked as many in an effort to find out for myself and perhaps for others what makes a drawing or painting worthy of being classed as a work of art. I have had in my time "basic training" drilled into me until I, too, considered it a bore. I have thrown it off, used it, revamped it, learned to fight its strictures, and returned to it with relief when a specific problem demanded its knowledges. But "First Voice" worried me. Never, in all those years, did I ever feel that I didn't "like to draw." As well confess that I didn't want to go on living because

31

breathing was such a nuisance! Or to stop painting because color irritated me!

Basic training, drawing on the higher level — let's think it over for a time.

Sketching in its ordinary, everyday, rough and ready style is not necessarily on this higher level, although it can be. Sketching, in its real sense, makes no pretensions, is not out to bowl us over with its profundity. It has its own merits, its own charms, as the sonata does compared to the symphony. Its very limitations and personal touch makes it a confidante of the artist who can reveal himself to himself without impressing or competing with anyone else. Those hundreds and thousands of pages tucked away on his shelves are his means of getting nearer to the truth of things, including himself. In these sketchbooks he need answer to no one, they are his visual diary, and we are wise indeed if we go to them to find the embryo, the inception and start of the artist's fully developed works. I have facsimile Cézanne, Braque, and Bonnard sketchbooks I wouldn't trade for one of their paintings if I had to choose between them. Have you looked at Braque's notations of chairs on his porch, of old felt hats, the people and things of his intimate life? Have you enjoyed a Bonnard cat, or a scrawl of a corner of the room in which he lived, or the tentative searching lines of a Cézanne tree trunk? Have you looked at a Klee scribble in the journal he kept when he was a young man, at a John Marin watercolor note, or a Turner one-minute scratch of his pen in bistre? Sketchers, all of them, and all with a basic training they absorbed naturally and soon forgot, without ever worrying, I am sure, about "higher level," and, more importantly, without losing the ingredients to produce fine work . . . keen interest, love, and a lifetime devoted to the joys, pleasures, and toil of drawing.

WHAT SHALL I DRAW?

At this point today, and every spare moment the rest of your life, with a pencil or anything handy, draw anything and everything. Forget the slow studied contour or outline drawing of the kind we tried previously. We will make rapid drawings, a few minutes of concentration in putting down a scribble that will catch the look and feel of the subject. This speed will keep you from fussing about unimportant details while looking for the main facts of volume and movement. Above all *simplify*. Whatever you draw has

volume, it occupies space. It has lightness or weight. It has motion, it is doing something; even the pyramids in Egypt or Mexico are *sitting* there, overwhelmingly.

Take a good look at what you are drawing. Let your eye and mind encompass all of it, not the parts. Look for the big line, the large shape, and then note its variations. The less detail the better. See where the planes turn, the forms interlock. Imagine yourself walking around and behind your subject; figuratively you are picking it up in your hand and examining it as you would a piece of sculpture. Scribble a line in and around these volumes. Don't worry about proportion too much, or if you find yourself distorting an arm or leg or measurement of an object. Get the spirit of the subject as best you can.

When people tell me they never have drawn anything and *can't* draw, I simply don't believe them. At some time or other, everyone has copied a cartoon, or been hounded through some compulsory "art" lessons in school. If you are timid about it — this is a natural thing; you must learn how to bring about confidence in your hand and eye. To draw can be fascinating and exciting — this making of marks and lines from life and from your imagination. With practice, it will become one of those acquired skills that permit you to do precisely what you want without thinking about *how* you are doing it. You will never really be satisfied and smug about the results no matter how skillful you may become, but you will share the enchantment most of us feel when we manage to "bring off" a drawing and know that once more we have made a little progress.

With pencil, pen, or brush, give yourself a morning of noting down quick drawings of things about you. Objects, figures, cars, fence posts, trees. It doesn't matter what. These drawings need not be large, but don't work so small that your hand is cramped and the flow of line made difficult. Sit well back from your paper, hold the pen loosely, hold the pencil between thumb and forefinger with the small finger on the paper to guide them. Look for sweep of line, seeing it in your mind's eye before you touch the paper. *Then* put it down with as much assurance as you can summon. Don't fuss, and don't rub out the lines. Begin again if you mess it up. Forget about "shading," accidental lighting effects, details. Capture essential form and suggest volume. Encourage your own calligraphy. Your personality will be written down in every stroke, wash, and dash of the brush *if* you let yourself go.

Behind the casual-seeming scribbles of the well-trained artist, no matter in what style or manner he draws, lie the disciplines of study and hard work.

BONES AND MUSCLES —
A page of figure anatomy
from a student notebook.

FIGURE DRAWING

Knowledge of superficial anatomy and bone structure, like perspective or other mechanical subjects, may be dispensable or minor part of today's art education. I have have never regretted whatever time I gave to these academic studies and traditional sciences. They were not difficult to learn and they gave me a sense of underlying form and structure that I have always found useful.

The illustrations show the kind of notes I found of value — drawings of the skeleton, skull, and some of the muscles that make the body alive and moving. We used to draw these from the actual bones, or copy them faithfully from anatomy charts.

It demands patience and interest to do this kind of drawing and some hours spent in doing so will help you to draw and sketch freely from the figure. There is no reason why this knowledge need inhibit your sense of fantasy, distortion, or other more expressive ways of handling figures — most artists who have done this well first knew their basic figure structure, as you can see when you look at the student notebooks of Paul Klee, Cézanne, and many other modern painters. Balance your study of this kind of drawing with the free approach and you will be in no danger of destroying your creative capacities with figure drawing and painting of an inhibiting kind.

A page of sketchbook figures.

Sketchbook notes jotted down while travelling or during informal moments away from the studio. Make pen lines rapidly to catch the movement and essential form of the subject. Seizing these moments takes a quick eye and experienced hand but with training it is possible to make notes that will be of value for more studied and completed drawings and paintings later, in your studio.

KNEELING NUDE by Peter Takal. Ink drawing.

SELF PORTRAIT by Diederich Kortlang. Charcoal and conté.

Figure studies done in varied techniques using line and tone — pen, charcoal, batik.

JUGGLER by Myra Posner. Batik technique.

GIRL'S HEAD by Matheos Florakis. Ink resist drawing.

HAZARDS OF SKETCHING OR, "BE CAREFUL WHERE YOU SIT!"

Flies, inquisitive children, curious grown-ups, trucks that drive directly in front of the subject being sketched, cold fingers, and irate landowners . . . Once I was shot at with a shotgun wielded by a farmer's wife, as I sat at the edge of a road outside her property. Another time, in Canada, in a small Nova Scotia town during the war, I was gently led to the jail for questioning by a red-coated mountie who thought I was a spy drawing the railway yards. I have been rained out, frozen out, splattered by passing cars. In Greece, children have charmingly presented me with fruits and flowers. In some places people have wanted to buy my painting from under my nose, while others tell me that their six-year-old child could do better. It's all part of the adventure of sketching in the open air. To anyone who wants to take advantage of the opportunity, an artist perched on his stool in public is fair game.

I was feeling particularly sensitive about this one day in a town in Mexico, where I had found a quiet spot in a plaza to note shapes of people, benches, fountain, the great gnarled trees shadowed and rich in color. I set up my stool and leaned against an iron post. In my pocket I had an official *Bellas Artes* card stating my profession, in case I had to identify myself. I had made only a few blocked-out lines when I felt a tap on my shoulder. Assuming it was one of the many youngsters who had come rushing over to see what I was doing, playing tricks with me, I paid no attention and continued to concentrate on my work. Another tap. I turned around and found a young policeman. What now? I thought, knowing there was no reason to be intimidated by the sight of a uniform. There was no law I knew of that said artists couldn't sketch. Perhaps he was just trying to be friendly. I went on with my work, determined to finish the design.

"No señor, *por favor.*" He pulled at my arm. He looked anxiously down to the end of the park where I could see the words POLICIA over a wide doorway where other policemen were on guard with rifles.

"*Por favor*, senor, the *Jefe de Policia* wants to see you." I reached into my back trouser pocket to get my wallet and the card. The policeman blanched, backed up so suddenly that he nearly fell over himself.

"No, no, senor! *Pistola*, no!"

I showed him it was only a wallet, and decided I might as well get it over with. I trundled behind him to the police station, trailed by a crowd that had collected to see the fun of a sketcher getting arrested and being taken to the *Inspeccion de Policia*. I was angry and in a belligerent mood.

I faced the chief of police just inside the open courtyard. "*Que es eso?*" I demanded, so upset I could hardly remember my Spanish, "Why can't I work here? What is the trouble? I have a card here which should convince you that I should not be molested while painting — here it is."

I didn't give him a chance to speak. I reached into my back pocket for my wallet and the card, but I didn't get a chance to open it.

"*Un momentito,*" sighed the Jefe patiently, getting a word in at last. "*Malas palabras,* no — no bad words, *por favor*. If you will just calm down, I'll tell you. I only want to let you know that your *camisa está sucia.*"

I tried to get it. Shirt was dirty? Then it hit me like a bucket of ice-water thrown in my face. I touched my back with my hand. It came away covered with silver paint! I stared at it, I flushed, I shrank to the height of his boot tops.

"*Dispense, senor* . . . I'm sorry," I sputtered apologetically. I grabbed his hand and shook it. I turned to the policeman who had brought me and shook his hand. I have never felt quite so ridiculous in my life.

The crowd outside the courtyard portals was grinning. I turned and stumbled my way out, trying to preserve some dignity. I would have rather crawled under the floor.

The Police Chief had spotted me sketching in the Plaza. He had sent the young policeman to tell me I was leaning against a newly painted lamp-post!

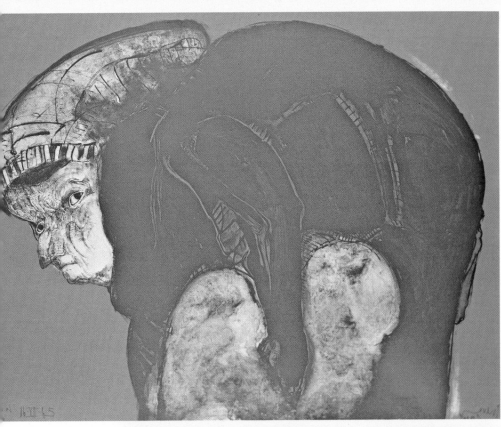

PROCURESS WITH MEAT by José Luis Cuevas. A richly inventive painting in mixed media.

ANCIENT AND MODERN GREEK by Elias Dekoulakos. Acrylic on canvas.

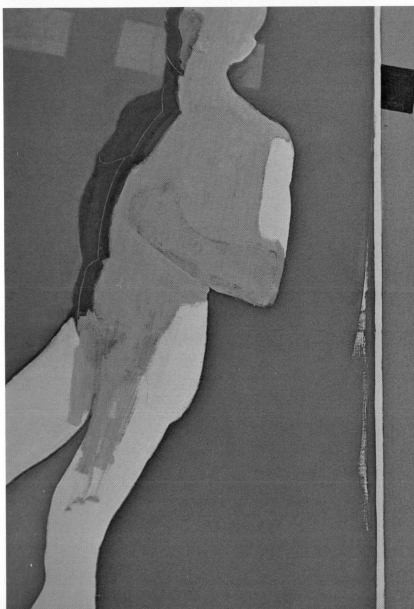

AN IDEAL "SKETCHBOOK-BOX"

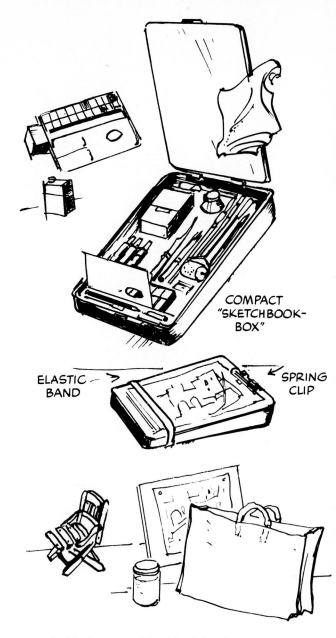

COMPACT "SKETCHBOOK-BOX"

ELASTIC BAND

SPRING CLIP

An ideal compact "sketchbook box."

After years of testing equipment for sketching I have found an efficient and compact solution for carrying essential tools and colors. Recently, during a year's travel abroad, I used it daily with a minimum amount of trouble. It can be packed easily in a suitcase, yet holds everything needed to set up a portable studio in a hotel room or on a ship. (Available from Arthur Brown & Bro., Inc., New York.)

The plastic container or tray has a hinged lid that holds papers clipped at one end and held with an elastic band at the other. Drawings, watercolors, and small studies may be made on it, and it serves the purpose of being a sketchbook and box combined. As shown above, it holds the following:

A small water-holder, the lid of which clips on the folding box of watercolors, which I refill from tubes.
Felt-nib and nylon marking pens.
A small screw-topped brass inkwell for black ink (actually, an oil-painter's turpentine well).
Sponge roller and holder.
Assorted brushes: one flat wide bristle, one small pointed sable, one small and one medium bristle.
Pipe cleaners.
White wax crayon.
Razor blades.
Paint rag.
Charcoal and pencil.
Sponge.
Small round tray for black-and-white wash.
One cake of Webers' Alpha Brilliante black watercolor.

The tray is not a deep one, lies flat, and all of these materials are spaced to fit in their appointed places.

For larger full-page drawings and sketches, I buy a thin plywood drawing board, carrying this in a light canvas bag, which also holds a miniature, Italian folding sketching stool (with back), an extra canteen of water, and an extra supply of tubed watercolors in a cardboard box. With this outfit I am all set for a world tour or a jaunt around the corner of my street in search of drawing and painting subjects. It is light equipment and once you have gone to the bother of assembling such a kit you will not have to stagger along, loaded down and tired, while searching for your motif.

For oil painting while travelling I use a standard 12- by 16-inch box, which, with some modifications, holds everything needed for oils. Instead of using heavy sketch panels, I have found thin acrylic-coated papers and canvases excellent to work on. These can be easily thumb-tacked to a panel, taken off when completed and packed for easy travel. One artist friend of mine did a hundred such panels on a year's trip. These oils — which he prefers to acrylics — were packed with wax paper layers between them and sent by air mail back to his homeland as he travelled. All arrived safely, and on his return he mounted the thin canvas on heavy board and framed many of them for his exhibition.

2. NAUTICAL ANATOMY

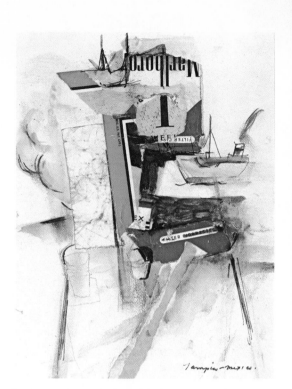

SMALL COLLAGES by Leonard Brooks, based on many nautical anatomy studies aboard ship.

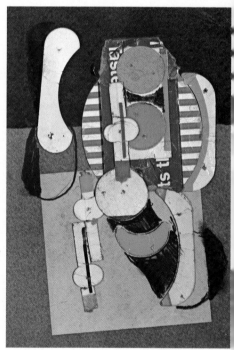

NAUTICAL ANATOMY

Vigo-Spain

Recently I found myself aboard a freighter taking a leisurely six-weeks tour of the Gulf of Mexico coast, before it set off for European ports. My everyday world became a series of long horizons, wharfs, and jettys, and the long intervals of throbbing machinery, loading and unloading of cargo, quiet days at sea, which gave me a chance to explore and study the nautical objects and machines I found all about me.

I started with life-boats, winches, capstans, and the high cranes that loomed over me as I walked the decks. Through my porthole I could see fascinating new shapes and colors constantly changing, forever appearing in new lights and moods, night and day, against strange new backgrounds of unknown (to me) cities and ports. Here was a chance to make a concentrated study of nautical atmosphere, studies I felt sure could be used and interpreted beyond the mere task of copying or recording the cold facts of commercial shipping machinery. I decided to make up a book of "Nautical Anatomy," in which I would collect the forms and lines of what made the ship interesting to my "artist's eye" — the muscles and sinews of pulleys, engines, pipes, and ventilators, which at times assembled themselves into pure sculpturesque forms and colorful patterns. I became aware of the subtle colors of smokestacks against the morning sky, the sea-stained green canvas on the hatch, repetitions of myriad masts and coiled hawsers. I was stimulated by the drawing and painting material that emerged from what was at first a welter of chaotic, cluttered objects. How far, I thought, could I take and use this material in a way more imaginative than the mere objective recording? How much study would I need before I felt able to free myself into inventive and personal interpretations of what I saw before me, before I could enter a real phase of painting that would have a true understanding of my material and would capture my ideas about what I had seen and felt?

I have illustrated here some of the first sketches in the development of my nautical experiences to show one way of "working through" the process of clarification, emphasis, and discarding of the obvious, in order to redeem what could be very ordinary and ostensibly dull subject matter.

First, the large objects and shapes — the boats tied alongside, the bow of the ship, the overall impact. Gradually we move in closer, examine with care the complications of a winch with its gears and pulleys. The sea and sky cease to dominate. Sitting quietly in our deck chair, one day the magic moment happens and the array of bits and pieces sorts itself out into a design; the light, the hard forms, the colors come together as we study them, and we rush below for our sketchbook and attempt to put something of what moves us on to the paper. We may make a line drawing, brush and wash, or add some colored accents with colored felt pens.

Our first week or so keeps us busy discovering new themes around the decks. Combinations of our anatomical research begin to fuse and we begin working away from the actual spot, setting up a corner in our tiny cabin as a studio. We spend a day in New Orleans and find to our delight the compact "sketchbook-box" illustrated on page 38. We also cannot resist buying some Japanese rice papers and colored packs of paper collage material. On the way back to the ship we find other material — printed

letters, signs, and posters, which we take aboard for later perusal and possible use.

The synthesis continues. We draw the shapes and lines from within ourselves, from memory and practice. We try to bend and remake the forms to a new kind of "seeing" and no longer feel that we must be bound to draw just what is there. That we can do this with some kind of authority is apparent in our latest work; we begin to know our subject. We have isolated what is to be of interest to us and left the rest to the photographer and illustrator. Now the fun really begins! And the hard work, for now we must call on all our aesthetic resources to refine and make definite our statement in the terms of the media we select.

A series of small collages is begun. Memories of evening ports, storehouses, neon-lighted skies over city harbours. Lines, colors, juxtaposition of shapes drawn from a dozen experiences merge into one. The final result is our concern now, and what inspired it becomes coalesced and lost in the new problem we have in hand. The creative process takes over and something worthwhile may emerge. (See Color Page 40.)

Line and wash drawings of harbor and shipdeck explore mechanical shapes for future collage making.

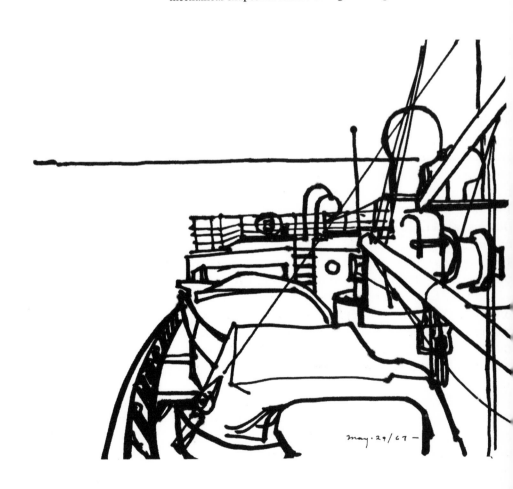

Marseilles Docks.

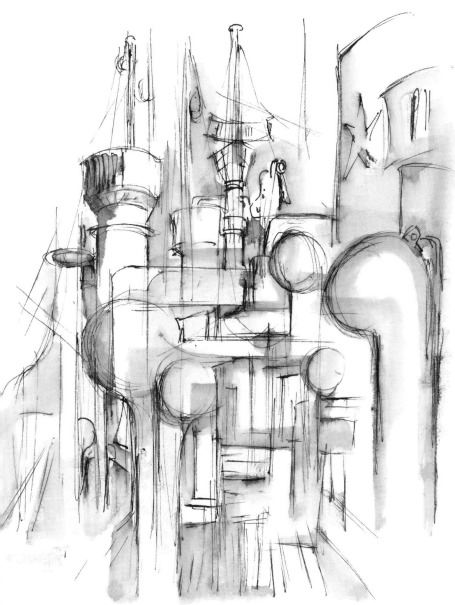

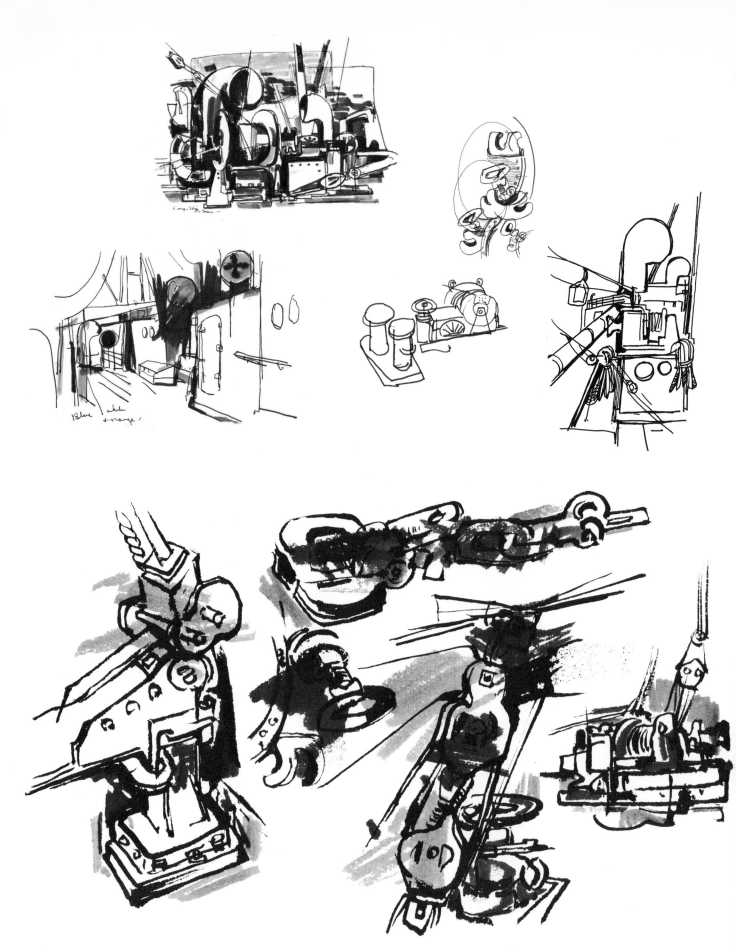

The anatomy — bones and muscles — of the ship analyzed and noted for possibilities in design and color.

3. BASIC TECHNIQUES

Wash drawing, 47

Watercolor, 47

Pastel, 53

Watercolor equipment, 56

Texture markings, 56

Some techniques, 57

Cityscapes, 59

The marking pen, 60

Basic oil painting techniques, 62

Acrylic painting, 66

Collage, 68

Graphics, 72

BIG SUR WAVES. Wash drawing.
QUEBEC. Wash drawing.

BASIC TECHNIQUES

Wash drawings

Painting in black-and-white washes will provide much useful training in your first watercolor efforts. The technique of wash drawing, limited as it is to tonal effects, will enable you to concentrate on composing your painting. Your composition will be clearly revealed and must be excellent. Later you will find the added color problem easier to deal with.

SOME SUGGESTIONS

Keep washes simple and do not overpaint too much — remember that washes *look darker when wet* than when they dry.

Work as much as possible with the brush — avoid pencilling-in and outlining first.

Save details until the last — get down large areas at once, lightest tones first.

Textures and variety of brushwork may be achieved as you work — use plenty of water; mix large washes in a pan ahead of time.

Keep the paper wet for soft edges and blended gradated washes.

Add sharp accents and hard lines when paper is dry.

Watercolor

Throughout this book the student is reminded that there are many different ways of seeing with the artist's eye as well as many ways of stating what is seen and felt. To one artist, trained in the techniques and skills of one special medium, the world appears differently than to another who has spent a lifetime working in another field. Yet both are producing art. I have spent many years trying to play a violin; I cannot sit down to a piano. Yet I have always felt that what really concerned me was the playing and making of *music*. All the scales and techniques were directed to this one purpose, although, as a small boy I found that hard to believe.

Once we have realized that the medium itself will create its own form, its own expressive properties aiding us to invent and bring into being fresh concepts and ideas, we will be eager to try new ways and means. With the exploration of methods and techniques unfamiliar to us we may discover new and fresh expressive powers. We will also expand our seeing, which has been conditioned by the constant use of a favorite medium. Certainly a watercolor artist, trained in the use of wash and color on paper, envisages his subjects in a far different way from the man who is a practitioner of — shall we say — etching or wood-engraving or who is a painter of vast acrylic canvases or oils. As an all-around professional, when need be he can turn his keen eye to the use of other means of expressions than his own, but we know well where he really feels at home, and his work generally shows it.

For the student, we reiterate, it is most important that he expose himself constantly to all aesthetic experiences, for in so doing the techniques and the experimentations with new media, in themselves, will help him and will expand his vision and *oeuvre*. It was Braque who said: "New means — new expression."

Perhaps you are a newcomer to watercolor, having avoided it as a lesser medium, or perhaps having heard it said that it was, in reality, the medium of the master, one which, after you had mastered drawing, composition, and worked in every other technique, might possibly be handled with some degree of proficiency and art. Perhaps you have tried it, and after a period of

MOSQUE AT RHODES. Wash drawing.

Two large full-page wash drawings made on the spot. White paper
has been preserved, essentials were noted down quickly. The whole
effort was directed to making a complete and finished statement
within the limited means of black and white and a few grays made
with diluted India ink. Bamboo pens were used for fine lines and
accents, added while paper was wet, for soft lines; added when
paper was dry, for crisp accents and details.

ACROPOLIS. Wash drawing.

RAND CANAL, VENICE, 1961.

Two watercolor paintings by Leonard Brooks.

EARLY MORNING IN SIENNA.

49

Wash technique.

Brush-stroke exercises shown actual size. Color dropped into wet paper, dry-brush strokes, razor-blade scratchings, large and small brushes. Try for variety and directness — without overworking.

futile splashing and daubing have decided that it was not for you.

Whatever your position in confronting this time-honored and difficult art, let us assume that you are willing to go along with us in our workshop and take a try at the watercolor experience, whether or not it is your first effort or a renewed contact with it. You have, I hope, already tried your hand at the preceding studies in wash and are now set to go full-out into full-fledged watercolor statement in color. Let us forg the relative difficulty or importance of the medium; le us consider its advantages as well as its difficulties,

ing it as a vehicle of your driving force to get to
work. Before we do so, let us examine some of the
background of the watercolor world, some of its
principles and its schools. For this will aid us in
approaching our own interpretation of what watercolor
could be and what it can do for us.

Early watercolorists thought of their work as
watercolor "drawings." They were minutely drawn in
pencil, washed over, and tinted. The English School,
which was to dominate later watercolor expression for
years, excelled at this kind of thing — and Turner,
De Wint, Cox, and Cotman began their careers

making architectural recordings of fine homes and
parks of Old England in the early nineteenth century.

Before this, of course, wash and diluted ink drawing
had provided the Old Masters with a method of
making studies for their more ambitious canvases.
Centuries before that, the Chinese had used brush and
ink for their masterpieces from nature. But it is not
until Turner's last works that we find the watercolor as
we understand it today: a medium for serious creative
painting, with the artist using its suggestive broad
washes with brilliance and vigor, dropping his colors
into pools of water on the paper, and brushing,
scraping, and combining his transparent colors with
other media. After Turner, there came a decline into
those antiseptic, pretty, academic works that dis-
credited the medium almost until the present day.

During World War II, in England, the great
tradition of watercolor painting returned to life. The
subject matter of the bombed streets, humanity
huddled into the subways, the rubble, horror, pathos,
and heroism of the English towns demanded expressive
techniques beyond the limits of neat, carefully planned
washes, or of canvases worked up in studios at leisure.
The artists — Sutherland, Moore, Nash, and others —
reached for their pencils and brushes and set to work.
The niceties of the purists in watercolors were
forgotten. Wax crayon lent its brilliance to washes;
black India ink, repelled by the crayons, gave intense
contrasts to the painting. Salt dropped into washes
reticulated the colors and provided the textures of
dusty bomb piles. Pen strokes strengthened areas,
knives and razors scratched through the washes and
crayons to the paper beneath. Opaque colors, gouache,
and white watercolor came to the rescue for bungled
areas of transparent washes, or were combined in
many forms of mixed techniques.

Renewed interest in watercolor as a serious medium
used by our top painters was increased by social
changes. Since watercolors must be made rapidly,
painters are able to price them lower than oils, and
thus reach more purchasers; for, while the great
fortunes have withered, the general standard of living
has been raised. Small houses and small apartments
require small pictures; the inevitable successors of
reproductions of the works of Van Gogh are original
works. Also, the direct and rapid statement of
watercolor appeals naturally to the modern picture-
buyer.

These changes are echoed in the galleries and
universities. Museums no longer consider a watercolor
a second-rate work dashed off by an artist between his
more serious efforts. Winslow Homer's magnificent
watercolors now make his oils seem rigid and less

INTERIOR STUDY by Joy Laville. Pastel drawing done with rubbed and velvety passages.

ITALIAN VINEYARD by Mai Onno. Pastel drawing done in direct strokes of lively color.

teresting. Sargent's reputation rests more solidly on s watercolors "done for relaxation" than on his retentious over-played society portraits, because in e watercolors he revealed his real and better self.

Today an artist may base his whole career on atercolors and reach the highest expressive levels. he great tradition of watercolor has been revitalized. is becoming a less specialized field by using mixed edia, and is rightly considered an extension of the tist's interpretative means. The purist cult of ansparency at any cost still exists, but in watercolor xhibitions mixed media and combined techniques of paque and transparent washes are accepted and own.

The possibilities of watercolor painting have not yet een completely tapped, and it may well be that some rtist will find and add new ways of using pigments at may become, in time, part of the ever-expanding chniques of today. The exploitation of the wide ossibilities of our medium will add to anything we ave to express. Without exploring them we are eedlessly limiting ourselves.

In the sketchbook-box illustrated on page 38, I carry ll the needed materials to make black-and-white ash drawings and watercolors in many styles and lethods. Most of the ink drawings are made with a umi ink, which I buy in bottles or grind myself from he cake or stick. Lamp black, ivory black, and other lacks have their own particular qualities and you ust experiment with these to find the one you prefer. have also found caked colors — large tablets sold

Pastel

The delicate art of using powdered color and a mild binder rovides the suave chalky velvet surface of a finely wrought pastel rawing. Opposite are examples of subjects handled with a sure ouch that makes the most of the medium. One artist uses the ubbed and blended technique, while the other employs the direct roken stroke method. Study the famous Degas pastel drawings of allet dancers, when you get the opportunity; if possible, see he originals.

under the name of Alpha Color — very useful for large wash drawings.

Experiment with all grades and kinds of papers, from the fragile Japanese paper, which must be handled with great delicacy, to the rugged thick handmade watercolor papers and boards. For your practice sheets, use a reasonably priced student paper with not too much grain or mechanical finish. Plenty of water, a large good quality sable brush, which comes to a fine point yet holds plenty of water when loaded for washes, a square lettering brush an inch wide or so, and perhaps a small pointed bamboo brush for lines and details, these are essential. With paint rags and sponge in hand, the paper at a slight angle on the table or floor — we are ready to begin.

Splash and daub, scrape and splatter. In one stroke of a large brush lay a smooth clean even wash across a six-inch width of paper, keep it wet, and drop in thick color with a small brush. Watch it bleed and run, soften and disperse into the wet paper. Tilt the paper and let a wash run down the page. Lift off the pigment with a sponge, flow it on, or scrub it on with a dry brush, using little water.

Learn to master some of the peculiarities of watercolor. The sooner you have done so, the sooner you will be able to concentrate on the more important matters of what you want to say with it. Don't worry about making pictures, or if the paper becomes a soggy battlefield. Let loose, make a mess, but try for some control and direction of the tools you are learning to ply. Keep away, at this point, from too many colors; use only one or two. Work with both objective and non-figurative themes. Learn the *feel* of water and pigment on paper by practicing with these simple means.

During the course of painting, stop, walk away, and return to your picture with a fresh eye. When you are working, don't be frightened by mistakes. You can usually pick up the color and water with your brush. Sometimes a mistake can be turned into a very interesting passage. Don't forget the trial and error method. Keep trying color mixtures on extra paper, as well as in your mixing pan. Remember the many little ways of handling brush, water, and pigment that you have discovered while working with one color, and try to discover more. Don't forget your razor blade for scraping areas when the paper is wet, or picking out white spots when dry. Use a pen if you want. Use anything, do anything that will add variety and sparkle under the control of your dominant mood.

Now is the time to quit. There comes a moment, usually sooner than he thinks, when a watercolor painter should be hit over the head, before he fussily

Roof Tops. Wash drawing.

Complicated subjects such as "Spanish Town," shown in the photograph, require simplification of the myriad details, and transposition to direct watercolor of accent and massing of lights and darks. Try this subject in one color or a limited color scheme.

River barge theme and a roof-top subject are used to explore black-and-white composition for watercolor handling in this manner.

Spanish Town. Photograph.

Barges Along the Seine. Wash drawing.

GONDOLAS. Watercolor.

Two Venetian watercolors made on the spot with direct and fluid wet-in-wet technique. Some linear calligraphy was added with bamboo pen and ink.

VENETIAN CANAL. Watercolor.

MARKET PLACE IN SAN MIGUEL DE ALLENDE. A traditional on-the-spot watercolor rendering from a market subject uses obvious and factual forms and colors for later interpretation of a more lively kind.

ruins what he has made. At this point, confronted with reality — which may not be intelligible or satisfying but which may have infinite interest, or terrific impact — your picture will probably disgust you. Take it home and cut a mat for it. Indoors, in a mat, your picture may surprise and delight you. After a while it won't look so good. You have begun to notice the pointless, distracting, unorganized, and unfunctional elements in the composition. You have found dead areas, sick-making colors and color-relations; the drawing and calligraphy are feeble, and worst of all the paper has an over-all despairing look about it, an anemia, or worse — a commonplace ordinariness.

Or is it really *that* bad? There are some good spots here and there, the textures are exciting, it does have a certain direct and appealing dash to it that you never obtained before — it *could* have come off. Put it aside. Do a pen drawing or an oil painting, promising yourself that before long, and at the right moment, you'll re-gather your energies and enthusiasm and go back at it again.

WATERCOLOR EQUIPMENT

WHAT COLORS IN THE BOX?

Choosing a palette of colors that you will find most useful, colors that will be permanent and mix well, is a highly personal choice. Standard groups of useful pigments are outlined here with some of their special properties. New and vivid synthetic colors are being added daily to the list of available colors. Many of these will replace the older pigments; they are able to obtain a brilliance and permanence seldom found in similar traditional colors.

Basically, it is well to understand the two main groupings of watercolor pigments: the very transparent ones, the more opaque heavy pigments that, unless used with care, can quickly sully and make muddy the mixtures of other colors. These latter are always used well diluted with water, not used directly in thick opaque touches. Such colors as Yellow Ochre — beautiful when diluted, and as a mixture in a light wash — will dirty the paper if used thickly. On the other hand, many of the transparent pigments, even when painted in their full intensity, with almost no water, will dry semi-transparent with a rich full glow of dark and intense watercolor quality. Let us divide the mainly used pigments into three groups, realizing that there are variations of opaque and transparent qualities in each color:

TRANSPARENT	SEMI-TRANSPARENT	OPAQUE
*Ultramarine Blue	*Cobalt Blue	*Yellow Ochre
Thalo Blue (phtalocyanine)	Cerulean Blue	*Cadmium Red
Viridian Green	Raw Siena	Venetian Red
Thalo Green	Umber (Burnt and Raw)	*Cadmium Yellow
*Alizarin Crimson	Cobalt Violet	Burnt Sienna

The colors marked with an * are the basic palette.

Cadmium yellow comes in light, dark, and a Cadmium Orange, which are useful. Cadmium Red Light is the most useful brilliant red. After using these basic hues, gradually experiment with the earth colors, the umbers, siennas, greens, or any of the watercolors marked on the permanent lists of the color-makers. You will soon find your own preferences for a constant palette suited to your requirements. Payne's Gray is a useful pigment for making wash drawings, or you might try sepia. From this list a basic palette for painting in full color could be assembled. I suggest these pigments, in tubes, of any reliable manufacturer of watercolors. Try them out for their lightest washes with plenty of water, and in their fullest saturation, with very little water. You will soon note the difference in their density, drying qualities, and brilliance.

TEXTURE MARKINGS WITH TOOLS IN THE SKETCHBOOK-BOX

Here are some of the marks and textural devices that are available to you with the tools you have in your sketchbook box. In this tray are all the means you need to work in black-and-white, wash, or full-color watercolor. Try a series of drawings using each tool or combinations of them. Some of the ways are illustrated opposite. This is your working schedule for this lesson. Perhaps you will want to work in your studio, setting up some objects to use for a subject. Perhaps you will refer to sketches and notes you have already made and wish to redo them now in another technique. Taking the same subject and making a number of different versions of it, both in size, format, and media, can teach you much about comparative technical devices.

Some hints: Don't draw too large. Use a good white paper, bond or semi-smooth surface for fine contour line, a rougher paper for wash and brush work where you wish to use dry-brush or pipe cleaners to produce tones of gray and textural mass. Don't saturate plastic rollers with too much ink or wash. Roll it out first on scrap paper and see what it produces. Shape up large swaths of roller marks first and draw over them when dry. Try working on tinted papers — Ingres charcoal paper is splendid; use brown or sepia inks for variety. Take time off to study the fine reproductions of the drawings of master draftsmen such as Rembrandt, Pisanelle, Turner, and others of centuries gone by. Take a good look at the new ways of drawing exemplified in the work of Picasso, Miro, de Kooning, Pollock, Jean Dubuffet, and others, and compare the differences in approach.

FOUNTAIN PEN

RUBBER CEMENT

RAZOR-BLADE SCRATCHING

WAX CRAYON-INK

DRY BRUSH

CHARCOAL

DRY BRUSH AND SPLATTER

SPONGE ROLLER

BAMBOO STICK

FELT PEN

SOFT LEAD STICK

PIPE CLEANER

Some techniques — wash and watercolor.

57

Marseilles - June 3

Place Dauphine

Genoa · Oct. 63

Genoa · oct 29 / '67 -

On this page are three variations of a cityscape done in wash, in Genoa: a small sketchbook note and ink and wash variations.

Cityscapes

pencil, brush, marking pen; thick line and thin. Opposite are a few compositional notes from many collected in many cities of the world. A busy corner in Genoa, a Parisian cul-de-sac, a Marseille waterfront, a bridge or harbor — new arrangements of subjects await the sketcher everywhere. Whether these are developed into paintings or not is immaterial. Their value is in *doing* them, to try new relationships of light and dark, of structural forms beneath details; to select and choose what you wish from the endless chaos of actuality.

Cities, mountains, oceans, landscapes — subjects to draw everywhere. I have often made compositional notes from a bus while travelling across country. All of these things are grist for the mill when the time comes to call on memory and the subconscious for design forms and free expressive painting.

The marking pen

Many types of felt and nylon pens for the artist's use are on the market today. Some are called "marking pens" and are available with felt or nylon tips, which make thin or thick lines. Not all are permanent; some will fade in time. In some kinds inks with chemical bases incompatable with water are used; in other kinds the inks are soluble in water, and a brushful of water over the strokes of color will make colored washes. Try both kinds. Worn points of felt pens can be trimmed with a sharp razor blade.

The watercolor pens are very useful to augment your watercolor technique, to add accents or lines. They are also inspiring when making free designs or imaginative "doodles." Examples of drawings made with them are shown opposite. The design motifs are made with repetitions of broad strokes of the pen, with dots and lines suggested by the materials being used. The virtue of directness is aided by having to put down definite marks and shapes that cannot be easily erased. The brilliance of the color encourages strong forceful contrasts.

Marking pen sketches.

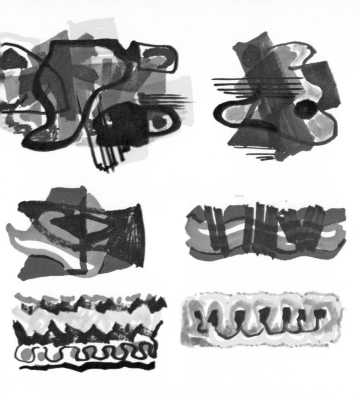

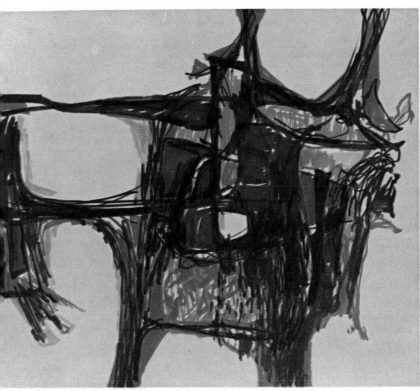

arking pen techniques.

61

Basic oil painting technique

If you are an experienced worker with oil paint these basics will be familiar to you. If so, you may easily skip the next few pages, settle yourself in the corner of the studio and go to work on the new painting you have started, or consult the project list for a more profitable session. For the newcomer to oil some information about the properties and techniques of using this time-honored medium may help to start him off without too much waste of time and paint.

Although the new synthetic media are rapidly replacing the classic oil and pigment formula, the fine art of the oil painter goes on in many studios as it has done since the first twelfth-century painter began to use it and laid the groundwork for the fifteenth century developments discovered by Van Eyck.

For our purposes — the introduction to a sound and basic technique — we will try only a few of the standard methods generally accepted for most contemporary work. With this foundation you can get started safely; the elaborate refinements of underpainting in tempera, the old master techniques of complex imprimaturas and glazes, varnish mediums and emulsions, can come later if you are interested. Excellent books of such technical information are extant, several listed in the bibliography.

Today we'll take the simplest approach, using a minimum of equipment and starting with the premise that you know little or nothing about it. There are methods of going about the mechanics of painting in the right way — there is nothing so painful to an old oil-painting hand as watching a student grimly mixing nasty messes of turpentine and pigment into mud and smearing it over a canvas without the slightest conception of what the color can and cannot do for him. Those sickly purples and chalky nondescript brushstrokes, which result not from control or desire but from a lack of knowledge and experience in handling, can be seen in any amateur show. This applies equally to the most realistic or abstract paintings.

Oil paint, as in most media used by the artist, has its own qualities. The ability to exploit these qualities, to understand their limitations, is necessary for any student who would call himself a painter.

The materials we will need for our first trials are listed here. These are the minimum tools with which you will furnish your sketch box. Later we will add other colors, more brushes, varnishes, etc.

BASIC EQUIPMENT
Large tube of White: Titanium, Flake, or Zinc.
Studio-size tube of Black.
Studio-size tube of Raw Umber.
A bottle of Rectified Turpentine.
Several hog-hair bristle brushes: spatulate, quarter-inch, half-inch, one-inch.
Several soft hair, square brushes, same sizes as above.
A painting knife, or several variations of palette knives.
Charcoal sticks and spray Fixatif.
Canvas or oil-grounded board or paper.
A palette (a piece of glass or disposable paper palette).
An upright easel — or you can work flat on a table for your first experiments.

Have you ever seen photographs of Braque's studio? Did you see the easels and palettes scattered about the room, each one set out with the colors for the painting he was working on at the moment, or his neatly arranged drawing table with the pens, brushes, and other favorite tools lined up ready for work? Perhaps some day you will have the good fortune to visit the studios of some professional contemporary painters and see how they arrange their workshops.

Such practical matters may seem tiresome. To the professional painter they are most important, and a well-arranged system of looking after the daily routines of his craft can save him time and bother.

Meanwhile I have described to you some of the equipment you will need to work in our workshop. Have it ready soon and let's get to the job!

We are going to paint in the *alla prima* method, that is — "at one go," allowing us to start and finish our sketch in one session without waiting for it to dry and without glazing and overpainting. This is the way many of our modern paintings are done — directly, eshly, and without complications. Thus the danger of cracking and later deterioration is avoided, the paint es clean on the canvas surface over thinly washed and iluted colors. The "imprimatura," a thin transparent urpentine "wash" that indicates the drawing and nodelling of the subject, is sealed in by the later layers f thick brush-strokes. Painting from "thin" to thick igment is the rule for sound and permanent technique. t is an ideal way of working spontaneously or for ketching out of doors.

Shown below is a 20-inch-wide panel done *alla rima* (direct oil painting technique).

To make such a panel, follow method depicted in igures 1, 2, 3, and 4, using transparent thin color, paque heavy brush and palette-knife work, and cratchings through paint surface to canvas ground.

Sketch in the lines of your subject lightly. In this ase, forget the face, figure, bottles, apples, landscape, r whatever and only break up areas into abstract hapes. We are concentrating mainly on how to apply he pigment, to find out the "feel" of the thin diluted aint when we add turpentine to it, to try out heavily paded strokes of "impasto" — the heavy paste-like igment as it comes from the tube. Use the brush to crub, stroke, or paint out smoothly the paint on the anel. Try the palette knife, cutting lines through the aint, or flattening it out.

Observe the intensity of the black, used pure and ith a clean brush; notice how quickly it becomes

sullied with white paint or a dirty brush. Try lines of black through a white passage; wipe the brush with the paint rag and rinse it constantly in a tin can of turpentine. Use a soft brush — pointed if you wish — and draw a dark line through the white paint. Wipe off an area with the paint rag and try making ragged edges or sharply defined lines.

Basic and elementary, yet how surprising it is to find that the tyro will often paint away for days without using these basic controls. The chances are that when you have done some of these things your small panel will look like a smear in black and white. The more you work on it the muddier and more out of hand it will get; the clean contrasts we are striving for will end up in a murk of dirty grays. Scrape the panel down, wipe it off with turpentine and start again. You will have learned how recalcitrant the oil paint can be if you let it take over. You will learn how to pick up just that right amount of pigment on the brush, how to lighten or change a tone without overmixing, and that brush handling has many varieties — as subtle as the violinist's bow-arm dexterity.

That is it. The lesson is over. You haven't made a picture nor even started on one, but you have learned some oil ways and the beginnings of a sound technique.

Try this same experiment with the addition of several colors. Ultramarine Blue and Burnt Sienna make a good combination. Leave out the black and use

A panel is developed *alla prima*, using several contrasting colors and white paint. Large shapes are brushed in first, all details and small areas are added as the painting develops. Stress horizontal and vertical lines, strive for a variety of textures. Use brush and knife. Keep brushes clean. Scrape away sections and repaint until you are satisfied with the over-all organization of paint surfaces. Avoid complicated forms for this exercise. Make the panel at least 20 inches wide.

1

2

DIRECT OIL PAINTING TECHNIQUE

1. Charcoal lines are drawn first, indicating objects or abstract pattern.

2. Thin washes of turpentine and black or umber are washed within the charcoal lines, after lines have been sprayed with fixative. Try for clean, strong contrasts of tones of black and white.

3. Mix white paint and black with umber into several small batches. Do not add turpentine to these. Brush in strokes with the thick paint straight from the tube. Try different brush strokes — smooth, textured.

4. Try using the palette knife to make thick impastos of knife strokes over brushed areas. Try cutting clean lines through the paint, and make accent lines in black and in white paint trowelled into the paint.

3

4

hite only. Make the darks with the two colors only.
dd white to each color separately, add white to
em when mixed. You will be astounded at the variety
: tone and color awaiting you. Continue to avoid the
se of subject matter and concentrate fully on pigment
andling and mixing. This is a purely mechanical
ercise; later you will be concerned with composition,
pression and so on. These are your practice scales —
u will face the music soon enough.

Try another 16- by 20-inch panel after you have
ied the black and white oil technique with objects set
p in a still life. Design a simple combination of large
pen shapes using objects from a table-top or shelf.
ry and match the relative tonal values of these — the
lative degree of light and dark of each object. You
ay wish to invent a two- or three-color scheme
istead of trying to imitate actual colors of the still life.
ombine a blue, an orange, with white and black or
erhaps a dark umber, a cobalt and white. In making
iese judgments of color and tonal mixture you will
on learn how to pick up the right amount of pigment
modify the original hue of your tubed color.
equired tones will be easier to mix at will without too
uch expenditure of time and misjudgment.

One of the weaknesses of most beginning students in
l is making the colors all too chalky, too white. This
partly from picking up too much white on the brush,
long with, as we cautioned before, using dirty brushes
lat already have white mixtures in them and sully the
olor. Another reason is the beginner's urge to put
hite in a color to lighten its value, forgetting that
any colors, such as Yellow, Ochre, and other
igments are basically *light* colors in themselves and
ill raise the light value of any pigment mixed with
lem. Yet another fault is to add black to darken
olors. This will neutralize and generally dirty the color
iixture. Learning how to use the opposite color as a
leans of graying and darkening is a useful and
ecessary skill.

Experiments made with these simple pointers in
lind will be very valuable to your technique of color
ontrol. Several mornings devoted to covering a
urface with controlled mixing and careful observation
f the results for later manipulation will pay large
lividends. Make a close-up study of original oil
aintings by outstanding painters. Note the differences
etween techniques — soft smooth surfaces, rough
extured surfaces, glazes (transparent stains) over
olors, rich impastos of thick brush-work and palette
nife; combinations of rough "scumblings" and
ragged edges, contrasts of soft and hard edge — all
he manipulations that are used to give variety and
orceful quality to the oil pigment.

PARIS, 1961. Oil on board.

Panel in oil and collage.

TABLE-TOP. Still life. Oil on canvas.

65

Acrylic painting

During the last few years there has been a remarkable growth in the interest and use of synthetic paints. Even ten years ago it was not possible for the artist to obtain ready-made synthetic paints that were standardized variations of polymer emulsions and pigments. Many of the artists who first experimented with plastic paints mixed their own pigments, using a polyvinyl acetate emulsion, which is a white glue-like binder, and powdered colors, an uncertain and hazardous task for the non-technician and non-chemist.

Now many manufacturers provide the artist with prepared tube paint that has an acrylic polymer base, or what is known as "copolymer." This can be used with confidence, as money, time, and the skills of modern chemistry have been combined to make excellent, permanent, standardized colors. Disadvantages that appeared when these pigments were first sold have been cleared away. Paint no longer dries up in the tube, color is consistently the same, and the artist has at his call many thickening agents, varnishes, etc., compatible with the paint he uses. The range of colors is extensive — Liquitex has thirty colors — and the materials may be bought in small tubes or gallon jars. That it has revolutionized the artists' traditional method of working is made evident by the number of painters who have switched to the "plastics." Everywhere I went recently in Europe I found some form of synthetic paint being used.

Basically, the techniques of using acrylic are not greatly different from using oil. The main difference is that the medium is aqueous and no oil is used for a dilutant. This simplifies the mixing of colors and is a boon for keeping brushes clean — a mere swirl and a rinse in a water bucket will clean them instantly. The main points to remember in using acrylics are these: Do not paint on any oily ground; most other surfaces are compatible — paper, raw canvas, board, masonite. Do not mix oil or turpentine with the paints; the colors may be used thinly and transparently like watercolor, though it is wise to add polymer medium to the paint to help bind the watered-down color. Thickening of the paint to a paste or heavy impasto can be done by adding Gel, a colorless paste. Additives such as sand, marble dust, and other inert matter may be bound into

SEA AND SHORE by Leonard Brooks. Acrylic painting on paper using thin and thick textures and varied brush work with some palette knife additions.

the paint with safety, for textural qualities. Modelling pastes can be used to build up heavy relief, but care must be taken to see that this is done on a suitable support that will not bend and cause flaking or cracking.

Acrylics have certain qualities and advantages over oils that appeal to the contemporary artist. Their flexibility allows him many technical advantages, apart from their quick-drying properties, whereby underpaintings are made and glazes applied in a matter of hours instead of days. Sharp clean edges are easily brushed over clean dry surfaces without the underlying paint dragging and picking up wet pigment. Color lies brilliantly clean and fresh, since brushes may be cleaned in a second after each brush-stroke. Mixtures of color are less dirty and sullied, the paint retaining a cleanliness and integrity even when neutralized; grays do not become "mud." The color lies beautifully flat, even when brushed over large areas — a quality much beloved by the contemporary painter who uses flat "color fields" for his work. Grounds are easily prepared by using acrylic white gesso, which spreads a brilliantly white surface for ainting on. New synthetic dyes and pigments have een produced in a vast range of colors beyond that of ne oil painting palette. Canvases will not crack or chip hen rolled. The advantages of quick-drying pigments or the travelling artist are obvious. Such, then, are ome of the advantages of this new twentieth-century aint.

Some of the disadvantages will be noticed at once s you use the acrylic. As an oil painter you will miss, or one thing, the good old smell of turpentine and nseed oil. The paint will not lie in brush strokings as n oil pigments and has a tendency to flatten out, in pite of gels and additives. The paint has a different feel" to it, immediately noticed by artists who have orked a long time in oil and know its peculiarities nd qualities. On the other hand, this particular acrylic antiseptic" smoothness has its value to the painter of eometric and "impersonal" surfaced paintings, where

crylic techniques. Done on thick gesso-surface watercolor paper, bout 20 by 24 inches.

ACRYLIC (TRANSPARENT) OVER MARKING PEN, CHARCOAL, PENCIL, ETC.

TRANSPARENT OVER WAX CRAYON.

OPAQUE WITH BRUSH.

OPAQUE WITH KNIFE.

OPAQUE TEXTURED WITH SAND, MARBLE DUST

brush marks and textures are anathema, to be avoided when possible.

Many painters use the stencil system of painting stripes and areas, blocking out, over the paint or canvas, the lines and shapes they want clean and sharp-edged. These stencils are peeled off afterward, the masking producing the distinctive sharpness of edge. Some painters use colored Scotch tapes and leave these as part of the painting, or they may prepare color stripes beforehand to be affixed to the canvas.

The possibilities of mixed techniques with the acrylics are immeasurable. You may handle it in a totally transparent fashion, paint it smoothly, churn up textures and high relief, or combine all these into one painting.

For a full and thorough exploration of the range possible with acrylic and related synthetic materials it is suggested that you consult *Synthetic Media* (Reinhold) and *Polymer Painting* (Van Nostrand Reinhold, 1969) by Russell O. Woody or other books on the subject listed in the bibliography.

Meanwhile, to get started you will need the materials listed here:

A few colors, red, blue, and yellow, in jars or tubes. White and black in jars or tubes.

A glass palette, brushes — the bristle hair brushes used for your oil painting session will serve, although nylon brushes especially made for acrylics wash out more easily and will last longer.

Paper or canvas prepared with a coating of white acrylic gesso by you, or bought ready and prepared.

Palette knife, paint rags and plenty of water in several cans or small pails.

A tube of Gloss or Matte medium and Gel for making textured glazes.

Plan out a panel of geometric shapes. Try a series of pigment applications similar to those you did with the oil paint. Flat, transparent, opaque, textured. Use the palette knife and build up impastos. Note the drying time. Paint circles and stripes over other paint surfaces, dry and wet. Try soft brush strokes and bristles. Rinse the brushes constantly. Work flat on the table. Try masking tapes, overpaintings, scratching through wet paint with a razor blade. Try anything that comes to your mind about ways of applying the pigment to its surface. This is the only way you will find out what works and what doesn't, not by just reading about it.

Collage

In recent years collage has become a popular and accepted medium. From its early years, somewhere around 1910, when the Cubists used it for experimental and unusual pictorial space and texture possibilities, it has blossomed into an important and unique method of expression for the artist.

Collage making is an ideal study medium for the student, allowing as it does a direct and personal contact with the problems of design, color, and pattern-making, which are so often more complex when working with a more involved technical procedure such as oil painting. A few pieces of paper, muslin, or other material, a brush and some plastic

Large collages in strong contrast, using textural variations made with spottings and with creased and folded papers.

glue, and the student is plunged without preliminaries into the fray. Large areas of color can easily be torn or cut, strong patterns and definite shapes can be made. Textures, variety of edges and shapes — these are all at hand and can be shifted and moved until a satisfactory design is made before affixing it in permanent fashion to the board or paper. Accidental and surprising effects encourage the imaginative concept, and the student will benefit from working with the large forms and simplicities of the basic technique of collage.

A few practical hints for the beginner. Stock up on a large variety of material that can be used. A "collage box" should hold many colored papers as well as white and black material of all kinds. Take care to use papers that will not fade, preparing some ahead of time with acrylic or other paints. Sometime you will do something worth preserving, and it will be a disappointment to see the colors fade away to a shadow of the original printing in magazines or commercial prints. Beware of colored tissue papers, which are usually not permanent. White Japanese papers and tissues dyed and stained by yourself will hold their life and color. When you wish to do serious work with collage test the papers and cloths you may use, ahead of time, by leaving them in the sun for bleaching.

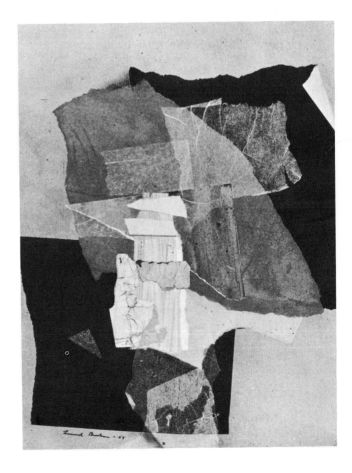

Large collages in strong contrast.

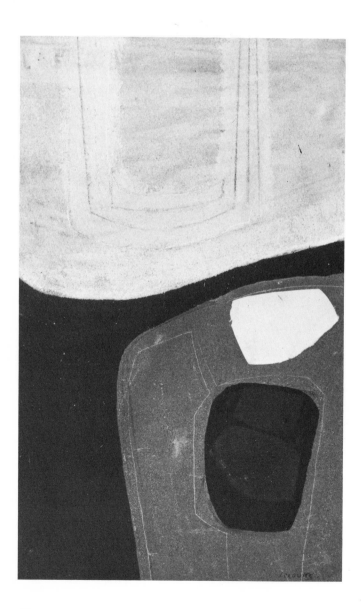

Collage combined with overpaintings and stains of acrylic paint extend the range of the pure collage. Such mixed media are seen constantly in exhibitions in works where artists have used the collage as a starting point for their paintings or used the brilliant surfaces of material as accents of color or texture incorporated into the final painting. Many of the collages in this book use the technique of gluing collage areas onto the surface of the canvas, then painting over them.

As a beginning, we will work on a 16- by 20-inch card panel. Assemble your papers as you would a jig-saw puzzle. Move them about, try to envisage what will happen when you place a transparent paper over a color, or interlock a textured paper against a smooth white area. I often use a small stapling machine and fasten the papers down before I begin the process of sticking them down with diluted white plastic glue, which dries transparently and cleanly under and over the papers. When I work large, frames and masonite panels are used to prevent buckling. In this way I have done collage murals 12 feet long without difficulty.

Reproduced on page 40 is a series of small collages made during my "Nautical Anatomy" studies. Here we see the use of material collected fortuitously — I sometimes wonder what people think when they see me scooping up a piece of particularly attractive faded green paper from a scrap heap, or tearing a well-worn moth-eaten weather-stained poster from a wall in New Orleans, Athens, or Genoa. I must confess the customs authorities were quite bewildered when they put their hands into the scrap-bag of potential collage material I brought back from my last trip. It was difficult to explain for what purpose my scavenging proclivities had led me to gather such stuff.

Work with a limited number of colors at first. Don't overdo the variety of textures. Try to construct and build from large to small, accents last. Add a line or two with a brush or pen if you must, but keep the collage within its own limitations as much as possible. Choose big design forms, as abstract as possible. You are working plastically, much as you would with paint, to make a statement in a direct unfumbling way. Use the accidental qualities but do not depend on them. It is easy to change and modify a collage. Keep control of it at all stages and make it obey your dictates.

Collage will help you with your sense of spatial perception. Areas placed over areas, recession of planes, and the influence of color and tone on movement into pictorial depth will become more evident to you as you work with it. Later, in a project, we will make some of these first studies into paintings, or develop their teachings into more intricate and fully organized "important" works.

HOMAGE to R. L.

KNOSSOS.

AUTUMNAL.

Dept. External Affairs, Ottawa.

Three acrylic collages
by Leonard Brooks.

71

Graphics

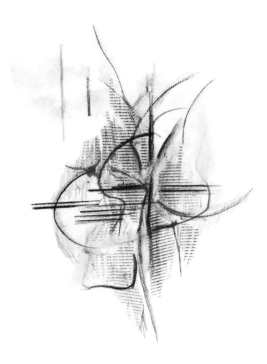

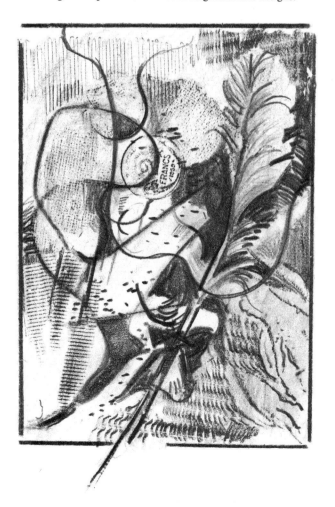

Rubbings on Japanese tissue from original relief designs.

Although you may not have access to the facilities of a well-equipped graphics department of an art school, much stimulating graphic work can be made by using the simple equipment readily available in your own home and studio.

Experiments such as the making of monotype prints, paper cut prints, and collage impressions will provide a fascinating medium to expand your drawing and painting activities. Surprisingly fine results can be had, even by beginners, without reaching into the more complex field of the professional lithographer and etcher. The methods outlined here are easily augmented with combinations of printing techniques, and the student should combine and mix these freely to obtain the result he is seeking. We include the elementary print processes here in our workshop to strengthen the sense of design, to break away from the routine of standard drawing and painting ways, and as a refresher to encourage imaginative uses of all the available means.

Mixtures of monotypes, thin oil paint on glass, stencils, and texture-making devices for printing in black and white and color, relief collages that can be linked and printed, the cutting and carving of intaglio blocks of wood or linoleum, all these will open up an unending world of expressive design making. The use of different colored papers, varied color schemes from the same plate, working in small or large format will delight you once you have begun to experiment.

TEXTURAL RUBBINGS

A preparatory device preliminary to making collage prints is to make rubbings from varied materials and odds and ends found about the studio. These need not be elaborate; the more casual the bits and pieces, the more surprises await you.

Brush a thick coating of white glue over a card. Affix string, coiling it into patterns, add a feather, a coin, or any small relief object that can be placed on the same plane of relief as the other objects. Leaves, coral plants, an old comb. Set out a design that seems

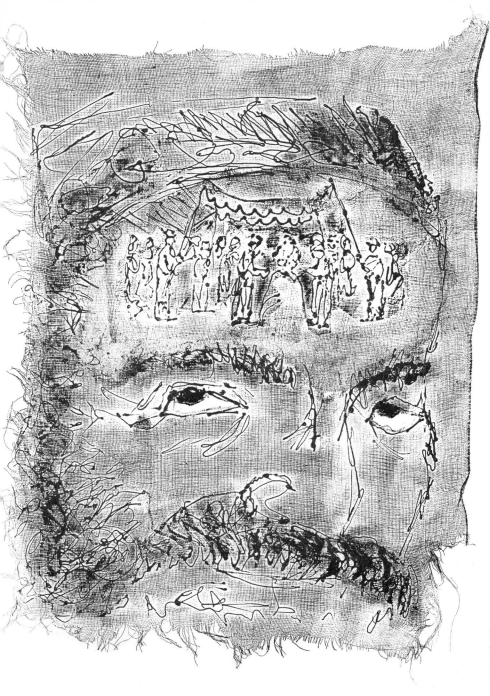

HODEL'S WEDDING by Saul Field. A print utilizing the design possibilities of textured material with free line to build an interpretive and imaginative concept.

have interest, contrast, and balance. When the glue is dried, place a thin piece of strong paper over the rd, gumming it with adhesive tape at one end so that will not move about. Use a thick soft pencil or aphite powder and rub the surface gently, building p enough pressure to make the dark outlines and xtures come up on the surface of the paper. Work om light pressure to heavy, lifting the paper to see hat you are getting and what you are missing from ur rubbing.

A trial or two will soon show you how to bring out e textures from the relief, leaving white areas of aper where you wish it. Coax out the design with accents where you want them, underplaying areas that should remain subdued. Try this with Japanese tissues, which, though thin, have strong fiber and can take a lot of rubbing and will expand and go down into the interstices between the materials.

Rubbings of this kind can be made from stone and wood carvings and any low relief form you choose. The ones shown were made with umber and black powdered pigment and the use of a charcoal stick, finally, to bring out the dark lines. It is much more pleasurable and rewarding to make rubbings of your own selected relief material, once you have tried it, than to make rubbings from the designs of others.

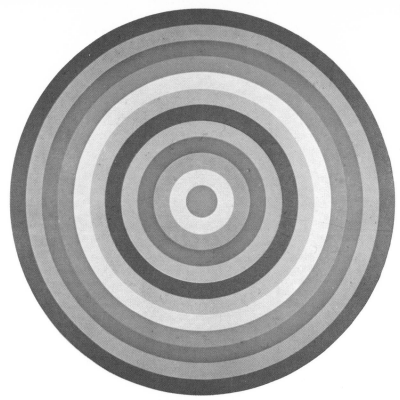

TARGET by Claude Tousignant, 1968. Acrylic on shaped canvas.
Gallery Moos, Ltd., Toronto.

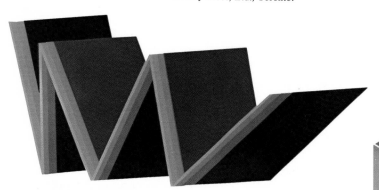

SILK-SCREEN PRINT by Gordon Smith.
Pascal Gallery, Toronto.

CONTROL CENTER #7: ALL AMERICAN BOY by Claude Breeze, 1967.
Acrylic and enamel on board.
Jerrold Morris Gallery, Toronto.

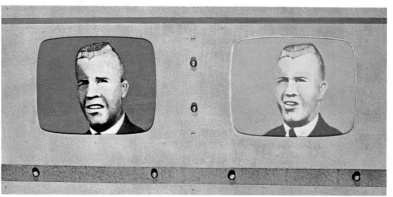

ARRANGEMENT OF ORIGINAL HEXAGONS
by Sheldon Cohen, 1967.
Each hexagon 20 by 17 inches.
Gallery Moos, Ltd., Toronto.

Shaped canvases, unit assemblages, colored tapes, maskings, T.V. screen, and free forms provide the artist with a new concept of format and the pictorial space contained within it. Horizontal and vertical boundaries of the traditional canvas are modified or expanded at will by the Canadian artists shown here.

For a number of years I have made "collage-prints," combination printings of simple means, as those given here, combining them with overlays of collage materials and overprintings from several prepared plates. Stencils can also be cut in thick paper and the stenciled areas of color superimposed over the print. Try these and all the combinations of media that come to your mind. You need not think of a large edition of a print, but make one or two with variations of color, pressure, and additional stencils.

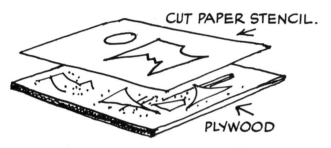

CUT PAPER STENCIL.

PLYWOOD

PRINT FROM STENCIL. →

PRINT OVER →
MONOTYPE PRINT
OR COLLAGE PRINT.

GESSO PRINTS

Lines cut and engraved, scratched and cut into a thick layer of precast soft gesso can also be inked up and printed. More sophisticated variations on this technique, using all the machinery of a heavy hand press with many colors and fine papers, are beyond your assignment here, but welcome the opportunity to try it if you are able to use the facilities of a Fine Arts Department graphic art press.

MATERIALS

A piece of plywood or masonite 16 by 20 inches.
Pieces of string, odds and ends of material, cloth, silver foil, corrugated papers, sand, marble dust, screening, etc.
"Elmer's" or plastic white glue.
Soft rubber roller, large spoon.
Tube of black or colored printing ink and glass palette for rolling out ink.
Varied colored papers.

Make a design within a small format. Use a thick card and mount selected textured materials, after shifting and moving them as you would for a collage before affixing to board with glue. When these are dry, mask the edges to a straight line with masking tape. Make sure to keep the objects on a similar plane of relief, not projecting too high from the card. Ink up the materials with the printing ink and set paper over it. Use the spoon or roller to rub up the design, lifting the paper from time to time to see what parts you wish accented and which should be underplayed and left lighter. Use a thin pliable paper. Japanese rice or mulberry paper is excellent, as it will expand and stretch into the furrows between the textures without splitting or tearing.

Try one of these with a lead graphite pencil, or with a cloth and powdered pigments, making a rubbing in the traditional manner.

With such simple means striking results can be had. Cutting cardboard shapes and gluing them to various thicknesses and printing from these can be useful. By merely manipulating good quality paper, embossings and raised relief lines can be made to create raised textures for printing.

MONOTYPE PRINTS

Monotypes are easily made. Any method that permits only one print to be made can be used. A simple effective way is to paint your picture or design on a sheet of glass, using oil paint thinned with turpentine or acrylic paint and water. To transfer the design to paper, carefully drop the paper onto the wet painting, press down, then rub the surface with a large spoon or flat object. The paper is then peeled off and a reverse image of the painting results. Pin flat on a drawing board to dry. An example is shown below.

Monotype by Diederich Kortlang.
Printed from glass. Oil technique.

4. COLOR

The choice of size, 81

COLOR

Color! Where would contemporary art be without it? Take away color, as we think of color today, from other great periods of painting — the days of Leonardo da Vinci, Cimabue, the Venetians, Byzantine, Rembrandt, or the early Flemish School; let the Ravenna mosaics be suddenly faded and only seen in shades of brown and white; take away the color from the Fontainebleu landscapes, the Pre-Raphaelites, the Hudson River School — and the masterpieces will still be contained in the subject, the descriptive content, and the strong appeal of black and white tonalities, the *chiaroscuro*.

But take away the color from most contemporary works, from the Impressionists and Post-Impressionists until today, and we have lost much, and often most, of the picture's direct appeal. It is only in this century that we have learned to think of color for itself alone, not as a kind of sauce that garnishes the main dish, the composition, the drawing, tonal modulations, and of course, the subject matter and its literary context. Today color often *is* the *main* dish, the force which determines for the painter what form the composition will take, dominating the plastic concerns of the painting and its spatial structure on the canvas. Color *is* contemporary painting. In abstract painting, color, which has been freed from its descriptive function, has blossomed into miracles of color sensations unthought of until the figurative vision was put aside. It is commonplace to talk of such things as the "rich and opulent colors of Veronese," the "gorgeousness" of Titian flesh tones, the suave finish of a Holbein masterpiece. Every guide book in Europe does so, and the modern painter, standing in front of the masterpieces in the Uffizi or Prado, is moved and bowled over by the intensity of them and the vision that created such things in the ages past.

Not until we reach the mature paintings of Turner do we begin to feel really at home as a modern onlooker at paintings, with the color world spread before us. Here we feel close to the artist who, in a sudden blaze of vision, threw overboard all the formulae of his day and painted, as though in a trance, a golden glowing world of color such as never existed before. His paintings, light saturated, textured, and alive with a radiance of pigment, which was to influence every colorist who came after him, are the beginning of "freed" or modern color, and no student worth the name can afford to pass him by. Light entranced him and opened new vision for his palette. French painters visiting England saw these, and became fascinated with the new vision. The "open air" landscape painting of Constable had already influenced the world of painting. With Turner's visionary late work as a starting point, the French Impressionists began their studies. Alert sensitive men like Monet, Sisley, and others went back to the continent to continue the work of seeing afresh the light and magic of a new vision that could forget that trees were brown, leaves always green, and skies blue or gray. Nature was suddenly to be caught in a net of a thousand new hues and nuances of color. A haystack changed its color delights with every hour from dawn to sunset and Monet set out to prove it with a dozen canvases changed with the ever changing light. Every season brought its surprises and its color recording. Snow could be blue or violet with shadows, light could sparkle red and orange; pigment would have to be divided, crushed, and assembled like shattered jewels to catch some of the new wonders awaiting the artist's transformed and visionary eye. Myriad dots of pure color from the spectrum, used pure or blended only with white, covered huge canvases as Seurat and others of the Neo-Impressionist or Pointillist school swung into the scientific research of broken color. This theory of small dots and blobs of primary color blending into a vibrating lively color at a distance, foreshadowed much of the impact that we find in later "Optical Art" color schemes. The cool grays and greens of the classic Corot were dismissed as limited and outworn. Color reigned supreme, shocking the traditional art world accustomed to the quiet tonalities of the Fontainebleu School in their somber greens and umbers. Red tree trunks, yellow and orange earth, green skies, green shadows on flesh . . . new worlds of color transcending all known recipes and traditions followed. The furious brush strokes of Van Gogh lashing his canvases in a whirl of color madness, even in an excess of the moment eating lemon-yellow oil paint from the tube, became a legend.

When this period stopped, the cycle ending, and the Post-Impressionists took over, the contrast was as disturbing as the initial color madness. Dark browns, blacks, grayed tonalities; structural, cubed, and geometric interpretations; the "rule which corrects the emotion"; hard edges, clean planes, a sweeping away of the Impressionist legacy, which had ended by dissolving its pictures in a haze of fuzzy color and little else. The early Braques and Picassos with their "significant forms" brought a sobering halt to the color riot preceding them.

But again the cycle changes, and it is not long before we see the first abstractionists returning to color, deserting the synthetic cubism and semi-abstract paintings of the Picassoists for a new form: colors, planes, and volumes freed from any realistic content whatsoever. The paintings of Kandinsky heralded the new wave of color, which was to influence every abstract painter of the twentieth century.

In France, Delauney and his wife founded Orphism and their works took color as a banner, using abstract paintings to exalt color to its purest and most lyrical heights. Color was freed forever from its confinement to figurative subject matter. Color became, like music, a force unto itself and needed no prop to lean on; it was no longer an additive quality to tint and define objects, to imitate light or shadow, or merely a decorative element of design. Color was at last redeemed and set free to function for itself, alone, as a powerful expressive language.

You cannot help but feel this difference when you visit the famous galleries of the world today. Moving from the nineteenth century salon to the twentieth is a jolting experience, akin to opening a window on a sunfilled garden. Gone the browns and grays and polite tonal schemes with a hint of a bright hue now and then. Gone the bitumen and umber, the pearly sky and green grass, gone the smog and pall of romanticism. How light and alive and gay the contemporary salon. Even the black-and-white canvases sing out with fresh and urgent contrasts suggestive of color.

Scientists will tell you that the physical basis for color is light. Light is broken into chromatic color, the rainbow hues reach our senses by energy radiated to us through a process of refraction and diffraction. We learn how some matter absorbs light and how other bodies reject it and how it was only during the middle part of the nineteenth century that man learned how to invent new matter organically, which would act as "colorants" instead of natural animal pigment such as cochineal.

We can also learn amazing facts about the way color is translated to us by millions of sensitive rods and cones behind our eyes and how closely allied is our sense of form perception with color itself. In any good encyclopedia you will read of the many ways man has tried to organize and break down the charting of color. What are its basic hues? Its primaries, secondaries? How can it be harmonized by the use of complementaries? Long and involved systems have been put together over the years by artists and scientists who have tried to pin down the phenomena of color. But even the best of systems have contradictory elements, and, when used in conjunction with an aesthetic pursuit such as creative paintings, are very dubious indeed.

Nevertheless, the artist can find some basic elements here and there in such systems that will help him to formulate a color philosophy for his work. Some nomenclature is needed for the description of color modulations and he will find it necessary to know what constitutes a complementary color or a triad. Black and white mixtures, the variations of color and grays need charting as tonal steps; experiments can be made to show how the influence of one bright color changes the color relations of surrounding hues. The mysteries of what happens to color when projected through colored film by spot-light can be studied; new lenses have been invented, not the traditional ground glass lens, but oddly shaped cast-plastic lenses that break up the colors of objects into entrancing new worlds of color beyond description. Color organs have been played, which weave color into ever changing patterns of light. All of these are fascinating and suggest much to the artist colorist, but the human element of selection and choice is still paramount, after all the miracles of scientific legerdemain are displayed. The color world of the creative artist is so intertwined with the over all aesthetic harmony of form, color, texture,

and the integration of the picture in its fullest plastic sense that color cannot be cut aside, torn from its integrated format and analyzed as a singular entity unto itself. Color must be conserved at the same time as form, for spatial considerations, and by the artist for its purely aesthetic reactions alone.

Can we teach color, not the cold and scientific mixing of color or "matching" of colors, but how to bring to the fore our *own* color sense? Is it possible to help someone whose pictures always seem to end up with a "sour" look or in dull and uninspired combinations of tired and spiritless color?

Generally we can *improve* our color aptitudes. Most of us have not begun to tap our resources. Often the fault lies in an incorrect conception of what color is and what it can do for us. The systematic dividing of color, chart-making, and a study of its idiosyncrasies still hold truths that will help us clarify the color problem.

Marcel Proust, as a young man, was asked, among other questions about his preferences, what was his favorite color. A wise and knowledgeable art critic, his answer was very astute and to the point: "None," he said, "for color is harmony . . ." It was the *relationship* of colors he loved.

As a painter you soon learn how true this is. Color, as such — yellow, blue, or red — does not begin to live its full active life until it functions *in relation* with other colors or modifications of its own hue. Contrasts, harmonies of modified basically-hued colors (the primaries), by mixture or breaking down into lighter or darker tonalities, apportioning of areas small or large, dominance of light against dark, the *chiaroscuro* — these are a few of the ways we are able to use color in an expressive and controlled way.

Much of this kind of knowledge is acquired, of course, by any painter during the course of his working lifetime. Experience tells him what "works" and what doesn't. He soon rejects certain combinations of colors or learns such things as why two areas of complementary color of exact size and hue have a way of neutralizing each other or how they produce a static monotony. For an abstract painter, especially of geometrical and formal paintings, a broad knowledge of color and some of its mysteries is imperative. Stripped of subject, intricate brush-work, imitative drawing, there is not much left if the color fails to function, and if the shapes and divisions of pictorial space so dependent on the color forms fail to integrate and come to life in the picture.

Much research has been done in the exploration of color in an artistic and scientific sense. Men like Josef Albers have devoted a life time to finding out what happens with color areas and relationships. His book of color research (a limited and expensive edition) devotes itself to the close and confined study of color relationships. (Listed in the bibliography are a number of valuable books that consider the aesthetic, psychological, and functional aspects of color.)

As a student you will find that much time should be given to this field of color research. Color help may need to become more direct, the few words of a master painter coming to the rescue at the right moment: "Is this green really as sickly as it appears, or is it only because the intense violet you have put near it emphasizes this tone quality? Would a *redder* violet help it, or perhaps the green should be made *colder* with a touch of blue?" Such suggestive criticism may help you cultivate your color sensitivity.

Actual work with the various kinds of pigments will soon tell you how much is involved in handling color well and with feeling. Knowing how to mix live vibrant grays instead of dead and murky dirty colors is an art in itself. Learning the way each pigment acts on canvas, how some colors stain, how some mix well with others; ways of neutralizing opposites cleanly instead of muddying them to nondescript flatness. Knowing how to take the raw pigments in all their brilliance and to use them with taste and intelligence is not easy and demands much thought, experience, and a willingness to accept disappointment when everything goes awry in spite of the best intentions and hard work.

Many scientific studies of comparative tones, complementary colors, etc., have long ago been standardized and formulated by science and industry for the practical purposes of paint mixing, interior decorating, dyeing of fabrics, and so on. Various schemes have been set up, such as Ostwald and Munsell, to list and chart the thousands of variations of hue, chroma, and the intensities of color. Books such as *Color, Form, and Space* by Faber Birren (Reinhold) are helpful in understanding color. Each system has its own nomenclature, which enables a color to be made exactly by a numbering system, and the obvious merits of this for industry is clear. Color wheels are available, which purport to give the exact and only harmonious green to go with a certain red; triads and complex color schemes can be made at the turn of a disk and color combinations of all kinds formulated at will.

Unfortunately most of these devices are of little or no value to the artist in his actual painting. Knowing about them and their workings and a brief study of their conclusions can be valuable, but the very erfection and infallibility of most color formulations defeat the human element of choice and selection, which is at the foundation of creative painting. Colors that should not, according to theory, be seen together may suddenly be combined in a painting with a far-reaching vision that outwits all scientific proof of incompatibility. Subtle gatherings of colors that would shock the color theoretician find themselves in close conjunction working happily together. Not a day passes without some color invention, by an artist freed from recipes or rules, appearing on a new canvas.

The abstract painter has all the freedoms at his beck and call. What he does with them is the measure of his place in the many fields of fine contemporary art. To be a "fine colorist" is not something that comes easily, even to the talented; there is always the struggle, the effort, to let the growth of the picture flower into something that will contain much that is intangible and cannot be too closely assessed.

Color, a picture surface alive and assembled with mastery, is still a rare and wonderful thing. Beyond the rules and hints, beyond the deeply involved studies of the scientist, beyond what may seem so simple and obvious as the putting down of beautiful color, lie the mystery and unexplicable forces that bring a work of art into being. If we could harness these secrets, list them in a book, run them through a machine, there would be no need for an artist or his work.

But the student involved in the problems and delights of color may expect only this: a helpful suggestion here and there, a criticism occasionally from someone who has experienced much color thinking, a comparative look at the work of fine painters. Beyond this he must step aside and let the human spirit take over. Perhaps with luck, something will emerge to make the struggle and work with color worthwhile.

The choice of size

The sketch was on the easel, still wet, and unframed, and I knew it was one of the best things I had done in weeks. John thought so, too, when he came into the studio to visit me. "Splendid!" he said, but lost no time in telling me what was wrong with it. "There's only one thing," he began. "I know," I sighed, "I know . . . it needs to be bigger . . . real big."

"Right," said John, "Imagine it up six or seven feet high . . . or perhaps done in stained glass in a huge window. Why don't you do it up into a big panel, there's that empty wall across your living room . . . try it in acrylic instead of oil . . . or perhaps blow it up into a series of textured collage and metal surfaces. . . ."

I protested that I really didn't want it seven feet high or even three. In fact, that I didn't want to see it any larger than as a 20- by 30-inch canvas. I intended it to be a small picture, and as far as I was concerned it was complete in itself and needed no blowing up or changing now or in the future.

John's passion for making things large was well known to most of his painter friends. Perhaps all sculptors have this urge to make things oversize. Show him a small clay figure you had purchased in the market and he would immediately visualize it twenty feet high — in wood, maybe, or cast in bronze on a high pedestal. Show him a pencil note for a book drawing and he throws his hands wide: "Now if it was done with a large brush and painted up THIS size . . ." He did have a size complex; there must be a word for it . . . Gigantism?

This urge to magnify things has paid him well in commissions, for it seems to be an essential part of our times that we must prove our importance to ourselves by outdoing ourselves in the amount of area we can cover. What the canvas says seems often to have little relation to what its dimensions are. The bigger the space we can take up in a gallery, the more important we would seem to be.

The problem of size is, of course, a serious one, which the artist must consider carefully. The choice of his panel or canvas, its proportion — horizontal, vertical, or perhaps especially constructed and shaped into odd geometric forms away from the rectangle and

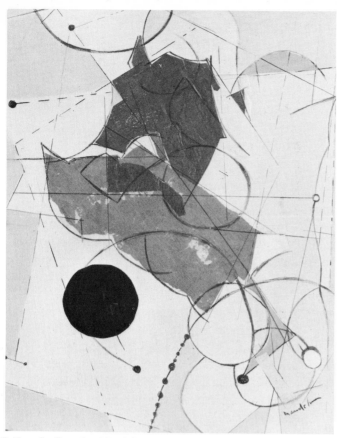

Collage by Beatrice Mandelman. 8 by 10 inches.

into the rest of the paintings, may become a dominant attraction when it is enlarged. Lines and forms alter in strange ways when they are magnified and it requires considerable experience to be able to visualize, especially in a mural, what the small-scale sketch will actually look like when it is on the wall.

Many contemporary artists have utilized this modification of interest and attraction by using the simple stark forms of the elementary shapes of circle and square and projecting them into vast areas of painted canvases. Lines and stripes, too, will take on an almost mystical character when thrown up on vast screens or walls. A dot is no longer a dot when it becomes five feet wide . . . neither is it a portrait of a football or a balloon. It assumes a new identity, and when we stand before it in a gallery and survey its simple, flat stark color field, it provides us with a visual experience that may be quite unique, subtle and worthy of our attention, if we are tuned to such forms of expression and it just happens to be a fine picture. It may also bore us with its stripped-away simplicity and we may find it impossible to read anything more into it than an elementary, if gigantic, demonstration of simplicity forced to the point of dullness and boredom. This is something about which we could argue long and earnestly, for there are endless theories, verbal fireworks, and just plain sillinesses as well as profundity behind this question we have touched on so briefly here.

The element of size, whatever you may think about it, is one that should concern you constantly, for understanding it is, in its way, part of your technical equipment.

square — is vital to his conception of the painting he will place on it.

Color and its impact and function is changed in remarkable ways when it is altered in area. What may be a spot of red in a small sketch, which is absorbed

GRAPHIC EUROPE by Luc Peire, showing artist at work. Black paint on white formica, 10 by 50 feet.

5. A GROUP OF INTERNATIONAL CONTEMPORARY PAINTINGS AND DRAWINGS

Structural space, 91

Six Italian structuralist painters, 92

An artist at work, 103

Back to nature, 106

Figurative or abstract?, 110

INTENTION B by Yannis Spyropoulos.

"Spyropoulos treads on esthetic formal organization and an urge to spontaneity, which is asserted in the occasional eruption of certain forms into stormy brilliance." — F. T. Ross, 1963.

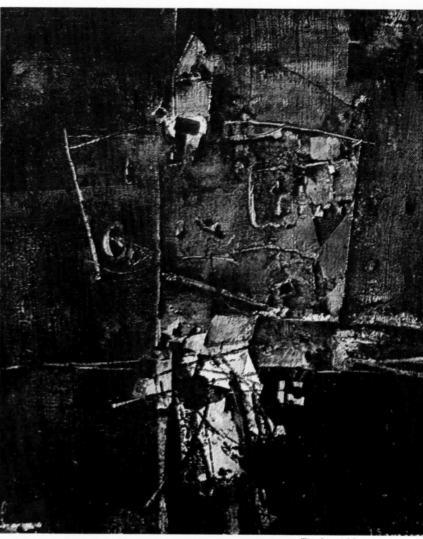

THE ULTIMATE SOLUTION by Yannis Moralis. Oil painting relating to studies on pages 86-87.

A GROUP OF
INTERNATIONAL CONTEMPORARY
PAINTINGS AND DRAWINGS

LIL, CABEL, Y ANABEL by Carlos Mérida, 1961. Acrylic on bark paper.

The first pen sketch, 1959.

1, 1959-62.

2, 1959-62.

3, 1963.

4, 1963.

5, 1963.

YANNIS MORALIS
Can a modern painter draw and paint in a representational manner if he wishes to? Here is a classic subject by a contemporary Greek painter who takes his theme through different stages, from the first pen sketch, which inspired him, to the final simplification of his subject. A series of large canvases done over several years ended with the figure expressed in a direct and plastic statement. By elimination, emphasis of the large shapes and the shapes surrounding the figure (negative space), and by a process of synthesis, the ultimate solution is reached.

The ultimate solution, 1963. Oil on canvas.
(Also see Color Page 84.)

WHITE CONSTRUCTIONS by Ghika, the Greek artist associated since 1923 with the French painters but with his own Greek feeling for the interpretation of his country and people. 1965. Oil on canvas.

The Innermost Flesh of Vital Space.

"Measureless fields of geometry where run together, attracting or fleeing, ignoring, avoiding, mingling, confronting, touching, joining, linking, grasping, welding, bisecting the hundred thousand directions, the hundred times ten thousand cardinal points, the twenty thousand ideal planes, the three hundred thousand privileged places of the most intimate flesh of vital space.
"Intersection points of contrary forces, fixed points of numerical value, chance meeting places; points dead, passive, aggressive, irradiating, sucking up, flying, fainting, pulsing, freezing, exulting; hurrying, slowing, diminishing; light, pressed down, dispersed; even, odd.
"Points alone or accompanied by lines, closed, open tangent, radiating, side by side; twins, in threes, in fours; progressive, deviating, squared, truncated; in parallels, obliquely, approaching, in groups, in crowds; haphazard, aslant, crossing each other, thrust away, mixed up, knotted, collapsing, trumpeting, muted, soto voce, superimposed; undulating, flowing, turning, cutting, transpierced; in flight, projected, deep down, skimming the surface, between wind and water."
——Nico Ghika, Athens, 1959. Translated by Wayland Dobson.

Night of Iguanas by Zdenek Rada. Mixed media.

Intention A by Yannis Spyropoulos, 1966. Oil on canvas.

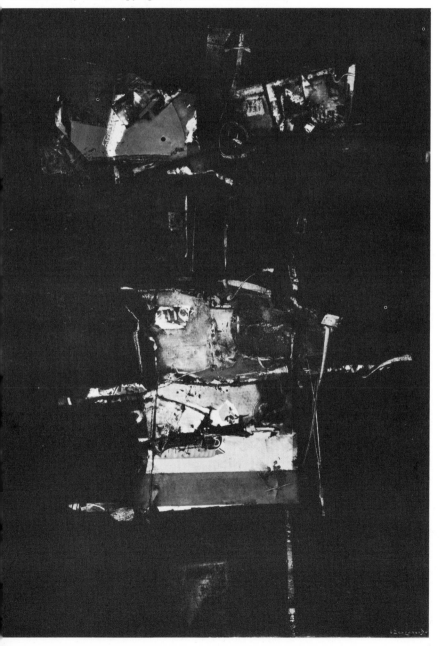

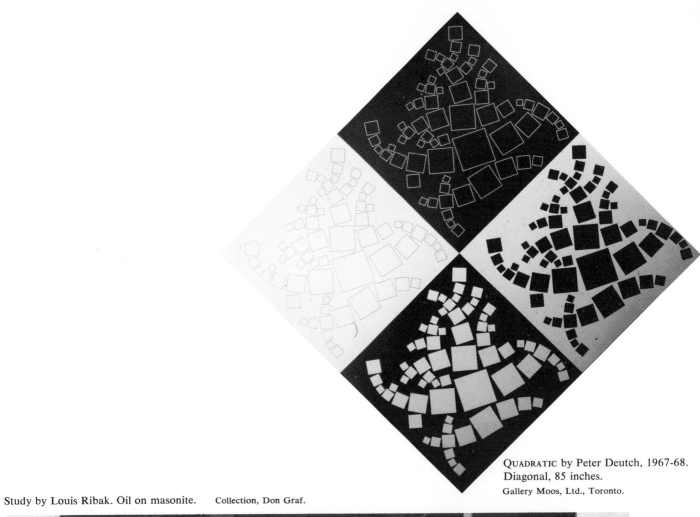

QUADRATIC by Peter Deutch, 1967-68.
Diagonal, 85 inches.
Gallery Moos, Ltd., Toronto.

Study by Louis Ribak. Oil on masonite.   Collection, Don Graf.

Structural space

The clean lines and spaces of contemporary expression are exemplified in the work of a number of outstanding Italian painters working today in Genoa, Milan, and Rome, some of whose paintings are reproduced on the following two pages. Constructivist in manner, along with overtones of what we now call "optical" art, the impact of geometric abstraction is a strong one on today's art.

The smooth, clean precise sharp-edged work of the geometric abstractionists has become a familiar form of contemporary painting. It has appeared under many names and headings, beginning with the early work of the Dutch De Stijl group in which Piet Mondrian was a pioneer in Europe in the early part of the century. Mondrian's move to New York in the thirties brought the influence of Neo-Plastic abstraction to a number of American artists such as Calder, Reinhardt, and others.

This is the world of formal values, controlled surfaces, and non-accidental qualities, which contrast strongly with the extreme pole of the abstract expressionist school of broad gesture and "action" painting. Textural brushings and surfaces are carefully rejected, space is structuralized, constructed; anonimity and a purposeful concealment of individual emotional identification is evident — most of these paintings conceal the artist; all, at first glance, could have come, at times, from the same studio and the same hand. Closer study soon marks the stamp of the individual within their closely controlled limitations.

Although primarily a European movement, the experiments by American and international painters of geometric conceptions — constructivist, formalists, structuralists, and other ideologists of the abstract idiom — have had a marked influence on many of todays' younger painters, who have extended the geometric approach into "optical art" and other branches of controlled formal and geometric forms.

There is something almost mesmeric about these dark lines and grids, which saturate our vision with large and empty space, flat smooth fields of color, rotating circles of concentric lines, and repetitions of geometric elements. And although today it is called

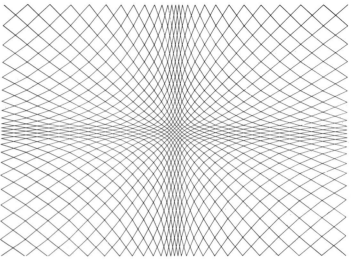

Rocco Borella.

"optical" art, this method, in other forms, was known and used by artists throughout the centuries. Illusion, *trompe de l'oeil* (fool the eye), space bent and twisted on a flat surface, with movements and flickerings of strongly contrasting grids and intricate repeat patterns, are not new.

Here some of the plastic problems of the artist are stripped down to the essence. Within this given form and style the variations are endless and the self-evident disciplines of the paintings demand a sweeping away of all the clutter and distracting elements of figuration and neo-expressionism. The starkness, the bareness of such canvases, may do little for you. They may seem easy to emulate. The austerity of the style may become arid, repetitious, fade into mere decorative pattern making. On the other hand, the optical sensation employed today with forceful geometric imagery seems to be a necessary expression of our technological age. It may contain within its austerity the synthesis and clarification of deep feelings, presented in a logical and orderly fashion eminently suited to our times. The impact of the work of these painters of clean lines, simple masses, and masterly design has been felt throughout the world in all fields of architecture and contemporary design forms, and all of us have been subject to some aspect or other of its stylizations in our everyday life.

Six Italian structuralist painters

(Photographs courtesy Galleria la Polena, Genoa.)

STRUTTURA E COLORE by Rocco Borella. Formica.

UGUO MODELLATO DIPINTO by Marcolini Gandini.

COMPOSIZIONE NUMERO 10 by Mauro Reggiani. Oil on canvas.

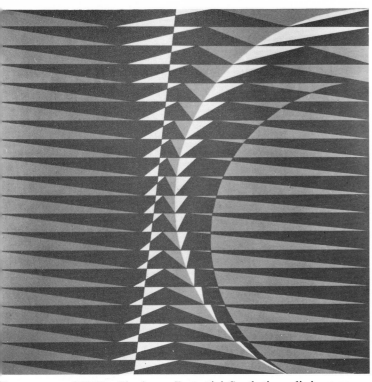

STRUTTURA en BX 5 by Gianfranco Zappettini. Synthetic media in grays.

OPERA NUMERO 13 by Gianni Stirone. Enamel on formica.

TEMPO SETA NUMERO 2 by Attilio Carreri. Oil on canvas.

RED TIME, collage by Beatrice Mandelman.

ROCKY SHORE by Ghika, 1964. Oil on canvas.

SUN by Zdenek Rada. Mixed media.

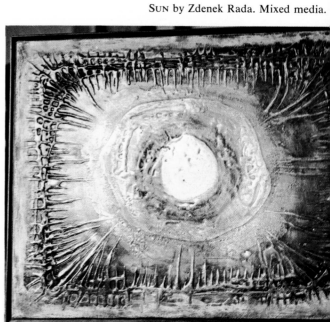

WHITE CANYON by Louis Ribak. Oil on canvas.

THE ASTROLOGER by Carlos Mérida. Acrylic on canvas.

YELLOW AND BLACK by Leonard Brooks. COLLAGE. Soft, "broken," and hard textured edges of lines and forms create lively sensations of pictorial depth and space. Layers of planes shift and move on the flat picture surface.

SMOKE GRILL by Harold Town. 81 by 74 inches. Carbon smoke and oil on lucite. Clean hard lines and circles contrast with the softness of smoked calligraphy, contributing to the visual impact of this painting.

ABSTRACTION by Vincenté Rojo, 1968. Oil on canvas.

ARQUITECTURAS by Carlos Mérida, 1955.   Collection, Mrs. Stephan Stone.

SELF PORTRAIT AS AN OLD MAN WITH GIRLS by José Luis Cuevas, 1964. Watercolor on Japanese paper.

99

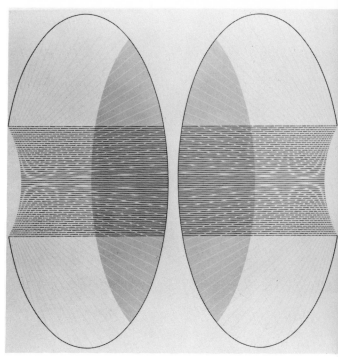

Drawing by Brian Fisher.   Jerrold Morris Gallery, Toronto.

ENIGMA, drawing by Harold Town.   Mazelow Gallery, Toronto.

An exuberant black-and-white brush drawing by Vassily Kandinsky, done in 1916.
NORWAY SERIES III, drawing number 12, by Thomas George. Brush and ink.

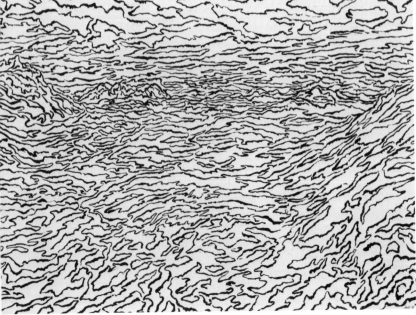

Drawing by Rico Lebrun, 1954. Ink on tinted paper.

An artist at work

This morning we are going to visit a painter at work in his studio. Bill has given us permission to drop in and have a chat about our painting problems and the privilege of watching him start a new canvas.

Bill is an abstract painter and a good one. He is a "pro" who has been painting for thirty years now, and there isn't much that Bill has not done or seen in the art world, from his early days at the Art Students' League through three years as a Prix de Rome scholar to his present place of eminence as a vital and important painter in the international art world. His technical ability, in any sense of the word, is tremendous. You need only to look at his early W.P.A. Regional murals to see brilliant draftsmanship and skillful figurative interpretation. There is a series of lithographs and etchings he did at the age of twenty-two that still sell. You'll find his early oils and watercolors well displayed at the Whitney Museum of American Art, in New York, and other museums, though his style of painting has changed radically from his pre-war work. Bill is, in short, a fine artist who has continued to grow and develop in spite of early success and accolades, which might, as it does to so many, have easily stifled a progressive and lively maturity. His work has grown richer and more authoritative with each new exhibition and there is a waiting list for his new work. His development has been sound, evolutionary rather than revolutionary, and when the time came to discard a way of seeing or painting, Bill knew it — and he had plenty to discard: knowledge, experience, a body of sound work behind him. He did not discard his convictions lightly, nor take upon himself a new personality for the sake of fashion or because of pressure from his dealer. Watching him at work we realize he knows what he is about, and the experience should be of help to us in seeing how, in one way, a painting begins and comes into being.

Bill's studio is a remodelled old barn behind the small country house where he lives. It is an ideal workshop for a painter who likes to paint large canvases. The overhead light floods the big, high-ceilinged room with an even, pleasant glow from the north. A long worktable, an etching press, a few chairs,

Action painting by Elias Dekoulakos.

several large easels, and some racks to hold new canvases and finished paintings create a simple workshop atmosphere, which has little in common with the romantic conception of what an artist's studio should be like — especially a successful artist's studio, one who is just as likely to have the curator of the Metropolitan drop in as a buyer from international galleries.

A large white canvas, at least four feet by five, sits ready on the easel. Bill is setting out his palette of oil colors on a large sheet of opaque glass, which serves as a palette on the work table. Notice how he has squirted out generous amounts of color from large pound-sized tubes and arranged them in orderly fashion on the glass. Brushes are lined up on the table along with paint rags, turpentine in a jar, and several spatulas and palette knives of various sizes.

We will look in vain for sketches or drawings for the picture that is to be painted. Bill believes in putting aside all his notebooks and rough sketches when he faces the canvas for the final version of some idea that has been churning in his head for some time. He often makes many color notes, analytical drawings in black and white, or suggestive compositional notes in charcoal on large sheets of paper, but he prefers not to refer to these when actually painting. By the time he is ready to tackle one of his huge canvases, the painting in its large sense is formed in his mind, although he tries to let the picture grow and shape its own final form. There are days, he has told me, when he comes into the studio knowing that today is the day to do "that red job," which has been haunting him for weeks in its embryo form. There have been a number of drawings made of the composition, in charcoal, pinned up on the studio wall for several weeks and studied from time to time. One day the feeling asserts itself forcibly — call it inspiration, call it a system of working — whatever it is, the moment is right and the work must begin.

Subject? It is evident that no objects are to be copied or used as a starting point for a semi-abstraction. No model sits on the stand waiting to be dissected into a fractured image, no apple will serve to make a modelled red accent in space. Now to formulate a lively and beautiful piece of painting; the paint itself, the colors, brushings, textures, forms, spatial relations, movement and synchronization, only these, and the understanding of expressive plastic painting remain. These will form the language with which Bill, or any artist of his caliber, will make his statement. It is a spontaneous and difficult way of working.

The large three-inch-wide brush is dipped in turpentine, a daub of umber and blue make a transparent and rather dirty mix, which Bill has suddenly scrubbed over the pristine whiteness of the canvas. Some of the paint runs down in thin dribbles, some of it is washed away with a paint rag, toning large areas of the canvas. A smaller brush is used and a few defining lines mark off areas of squares and circular forms.

For some of us, this is the hardest part of painting, worse than jumping into ice-cold water. Beginning a page of writing is similar: to get started, to generate steam, to destroy that smug white paper or canvas, which is going to be the scene of a fine battle as the engagement continues — one that will end in the domination of the material or else be scrapped. Taking a defiant swing at the very outset of the battle is a good psychological thing to do. Get something on the staring white canvas, destroy the surface; get down a starting sentence, get under way. These beginnings can always be removed, covered over, or lost in the final version.

For the abstract painter, the beginning is even more important than for the traditional worker. These first strokes are the beginnings of an organic growth. You will be wise to watch the first markings Bill is making on his canvas. Many painters go about it differently, but it adds up to the same thing, the struggle to overcome nothingness, to invent, control, subdue, bring to life, assemble, to make function; to bring into being something that did not exist before, and to capture within its medium some of the energy that comes out of the end of a brush.

"But anyone can do that," you may think as you watch the raw stroke of umber cross another, an accidental blob of blue falling away from a right-hand corner, the dabs, strokes, and varied brushings practically controlling themselves. So it may seem for the moment, but watch the painting as it grows more complex, watch those apparently accidental touches and manipulations of the brush. Skills from many years of brush-wielding lie behind the twirl of the palette knife, the slash of a bristle. Watch the broken stroke that flips across an area in such a way that the stroke breaks on one side and forms an even hard edge on the other; observe a line grow from thin to thick, cutting into the textured red, which is forming an off-center accent now. No timid drawing, no futile scraping, no "fancy" brush work. Each stroke finds its inevitable place, each color comes on the scene as it is called for. Beneath what may look like chaos and mess lies a direction as right and as preordained as the trained fingers of a virtuoso violinist hitting a high G without hesitancy or a flaw.

An energetic half-hour has gone by during which Bill has covered his canvas, scraped out a passage or two, repainted sections, and stopped to step back and see what the painting looks like from ten feet or so. Several times he has taken the canvas and turned it upside down and sideways, to consider its general impact, though it is obvious that there is no need to do this to obliterate the figuration of objects, as a figurative painter will often do when he desires to see the colors and forms alone, freed from their content.

If the concentrated effort of keeping the canvas going in all of its parts, adjusting color, and form against form, is tiring for the artist, it is equally so for the onlooker. It is time to set aside the painting in progress, and to relax. Completed or not, the once white space on the easel is now a dancing area of beautifully modulated color intermingling in sparkling contrasts of shapes, horizontal and vertical, joined by thin overwritings of thread-like black lines. The dirty umber-blue underpainting has disappeared and the thicker lime-yellow and orange pigment brushed over it has the delightful fragile quality of vibrating butterfly wings. Our eye moves over the canvas, passing from accent to accent, from flat simple areas to busy and agitated ones. The canvas is radiant with its own light, color, and forms in space. Do you not feel some of its mystery and appeal? Or will you demand of the artist a "recognizable" object? Have you learned to like and how to "read" a painting that has cast out the unneeded elements and has been painted from deep within the artist's self, which Herbert Read has called "the paintings of Inner Necessity"?

HOUSES AT ARGENTEUIL by Nicholas de Staël. Oil on canvas. (Reproduced actual size.)

RUSSIAN CIRCUS, collage by Leonard Brooks.

There are many questions we would like to ask. They are the inevitable ones that come from an honest confusion about what an abstract painter is trying to do, from the misunderstandings of what abstraction is, what it strives for, its fundamental differences from what has been accepted and is traditionally understood. Some of these questions are answered in this book. Some of them are unanswerable except with a paint brush.

You will recognize Bill's painting in an exhibition because it will breathe a life of its own, will "feel" right. It will be honest, give off the savor of integrity; there will be no doubts about it when you come across such works. They will be, like other genuine expressions of a creative personality, stamped in every touch — figurative or abstract — as another of those mysterious and cherished objects in a tired world — a work of art.

Back to nature

You will always find it a stimulating and refreshing experience to look to nature for subjects to draw and paint. One of the geometric painters I know draws faithfully from life every week, and many abstract painters find inspiration in drawing from the natural forms of plants and landscapes. A close look at a bee, a spider web, the textures on the back surface of a sycamore tree, a cloud formation — all of these will provide design and color themes to renew a tired and repetitious eye and hand.

BIRDS IN THE RAIN by Anna Wu Weakland. Oriental brush work interprets two birds with skillful summing up of washes and brush textures of a traditional kind.

FEB 19. 62

POPPIES by Peter Takal, 1968. Pen and ink on prepared ground.

Nature study by Herbert Stansfield. A careful, almost botanical pencil drawing explores the leaf structure of a plant with loving detail. Made with Durer-like precision many years ago by one of my early instructors.

FISHES by Peter Takal, 1967. Pen and ink on prepared ground.

Drawing by Sylvia Tate. Wax crayon, ink, line, and wash are used to make this imaginative complex texture of all-over patterning.

BEE by Mai Onno. The artist studies the configurations of a bee in close-up focus to make an exciting drawing from nature.

Figurative or abstract?

Shown on this page is a group of semi-abstract subjects using figurative material. All of these are used to build organized compositions that use overlapping planes and "fracturing" of the image to strengthen the design. Large areas, small accents of color, light and dark sections organized to fill the pictorial space of the flat surface. Compare this approach to the purer abstract conception of free forms in the group shown opposite.

Here the figuration is purely inventive. The depiction of objects and semi-abstraction of subject matter is rejected. Only the forms and spaces, textures and colors are used to make a pure direct structure to please the visual sense — a new reality is created using shapes and sometimes symbols to form the painting. Interest is sustained without recall of place or thing. Such an approach takes knowledge, sensitivity, and an understanding of pictorial space. There are no props to lean on, and no message is presented by the painting in itself.

CATHEDRAL IN VENICE. Oil on canvas.

TABLE-TOP COLLAGE.

GREEK ISLAND HARBOR. Oil on canvas.

Abstract motifs done in oil, collage, acrylics, combinations, and mixed techniques. Allover texture and varied surfaces are created with palette knife, marble dust, and paper and cloth material. Only design, texture, and color are used to make a statement. There is no reference to place or thing.

KABUKI by York Wilson. Acrylic.

TEMPO DELTA No. 11 by Attilio Carreri. Oil on canvas.

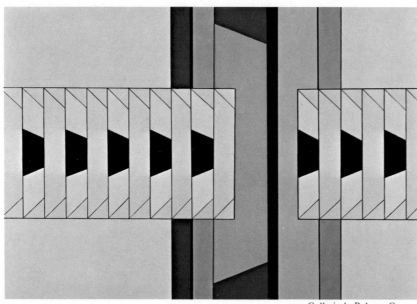

Galleria la Polena, Genoa.

6. A SCHEDULE FOR PAINTER'S WORKSHOP

Checklist of subjects to be studied, 114

Basic techniques and materials, 115

Twenty-five projects, 115

A SCHEDULE FOR PAINTER'S WORKSHOP
Check list of subjects to be studied

Here is a listing of subjects for our Workshop sessions. Some will be familiar to you, others new and unexplored. Use *the removable Painter's Workshop Chart and Schedule of Twenty-five Projects* at the end of this book to help you plan your periods of study. Pin it up in your studio and check off your progress, remembering that the suggested material is planned to help you find your own style and manner of working, your own personal expression. Rules and theories are made to be broken at will, but true creativity will only come from many experiences and experiments in the countless ways of working open to you. Augment the suggested projects with research in depth. Start a file of illustrations relevant to your project. Consult the bibliography for books that consider your problem. At all times, balance the practical matters of technique with the vitality and personal quality of your own thinking and seeing.

Some drawing ways

Exploratory drawings: Outline in fine pen line, contour studies, slow careful brush and pen observations to train mind and hand. Many such.

Trial techniques: Use and learn various tools, traditional and unorthodox as listed in the book. Black and white only, pipe cleaners, bamboo pen, rollers. Collect reproductions of drawings by master draftsmen.

Investigate elementary perspective books and theories: Projection of solids, cube, cone, cylinder. Up- and down-hill perspective. Drawings of streets, objects from photographs and objects traced and analyzed.

Study of non-perspective renderings: by Oriental and Byzantine artists. Space projection without receding parallels to vanishing point. A look at Cubist experiments. Gris, Braque, Feininger.

Picture plane and its problems: limited space, shallow and deep space; Cézanne projection of solids. Planes controlled in pictorial space by flattening of depth using horizontal and vertical emphasis.

Negative and dynamic space and spatial concepts: Movement in pictorial depth versus surface movement. Organization of shapes in picture plane.

Compositional devices: Basic design and understanding of visual forms. Repetition, rhythm, contrast, dominance, etc. Dynamic energies of these forms — curves, horizontal, diagonal; vertical, zig-zag, spottings, etc. Enclose these in various format: square, rectangular, circular.

Further compositional studies: A few objects analyzed in black and white, within a rectangular border. Linear flow of line, spotting of black and white mass, balance and counter balance. Movement, thrusts, and tensions set up with regard to interval and repetition of marks, spots, and linear flow through composition.

Theory forgotten: Free drawings made from subjects out-of-doors. Choose simple large shapes and try versions of black and white, pure line and tonal interpretations. Sketch-book morning to collect ideas for further development.

Figure drawing: Contour and gesture drawing of quick notations from life. Free models everywhere. Some pages of these notes with no attempt to make finished studies. The same with animal or bird forms.

Some studio study of anatomy: From skeleton and skull photos or drawings. Structure and proportion. Artists' anatomy book from library.

Imaginative drawings: Of figure made after bones and muscle study. Freely drawn and expressive, distorted or exaggerated as much as you wish.

Nature study: Flowers, branches, fruit and leaves; bees, goldfish, or the design in a sliced tomato. Careful drawings in pencil, ink, color to understand organic growth and structure of natural forms.

Basic techniques and materials

Wash drawing: Black and white tonal exercises in control of brush; washes, dry-brush, textures. Judging light and dark values. Pointed, flat, small, and large brushes. Various papers and their qualities.

Watercolor: Continued experiments in one, two and more colors. Trial of various colors for transparent and opaque properties. Intensity of hue, dilution, mixtures of colors. Non-representational studies to explore brilliance of color, textures, etc.

Watercolor pinned down to objects of simple kind, two bottles and a pear, etc. Dry paper, wet paper, combination of both. Trial of razor-blade and knife-scratchings, sponge, roller. Direct brushwork, work with fixed charcoal lines and pencil preliminaries.

study out-of-doors: Strong composition first, simple washes, some pen strokes added last. A "take-what-you-need" project. Re-do in studio. Watercolor transparent or with opaque touches, casein or gouache.

Crayon, oil and pastel: Studio work with free design forms and pattern making. Work on tinted papers and white. Shun literal copying and invent non-objective compositions.

Marking pens: As above. Brown, black used in thick and thin line, dry and wet. Colored pens combined. Watercolor pens used and diluted for washes. Combine watercolor paintings and lines made by pens.

Oil painting: Basic qualities explored as in book. Imprimatura, over-painting in brush, thick and thin. Use of turpentine. Turpentine and linseed oil. Glazes in transparent color. Thick underpainting with quick-drying white. Palette knife work. Work in black and white or umber and white only.

More oil techniques. Heavy impasto, "scumbling" paint over dry areas. Work to develop "feel" of paint in all its qualities. Add two colors and paint out dark and light range. Different brushes — sable and hog-hair; different painting knives — spatulate, diamond shape, etc. A 16- by 20-inch canvas. Limited palette. Painting from group of objects used only to suggest composition of textures and shapes. A morning's work — to draw, paint, and complete it "alla prima."

Oil used in tight geometric fashion making simple open pattern and color version similar to structuralist painters in book.

Acrylics: Trials as described in book. Paper and acrylic-gessoed canvas. Seek out further information on this media. Try in transparent and opaque methods.

Collage: Three colors. Texture trial. Transparent papers. Abstract forms only to be used, the larger and non-complex, the better. Study Schwitters, Motherwell, and others in reproduction.

Graphics: Textural rubbings as in book. Simple print-making stencil collage-prints, plaster prints, monotype. Investigate further techniques as used by print-makers today.

Assemblage and Collage: Panel made with collage background and mounted objects; textures and three-dimensional forms. Color with acrylics.

Found objects: Gather together interesting natural forms, stones, driftwood, bones or what have you. Selection for sculpturesque appeal. Mount in a box or on pedestal. Make drawings from these.

A morning of recapitulation: An examination and self-criticism of work done and in process. A setting aside of the best for further development. A session of contemplation and thought and a look at your own progress and failures.

Twenty-five projects

Below is a list of twenty-five projects for you to do, described and illustrated on the pages that follow. They range over many different techniques and approaches. Try them all, checking off each session on your Workshop Pin-up Chart. Choose a project that appeals to you at the moment. It is not necessary to follow the projects in the order outlined.

Project 1. Contour drawings from nature.
Project 2. Perspective used and dismissed.
Project 3. Direct drawings from nature.
Project 4. Salvaging a "dud."
Project 5. A poster for your exhibition.
Project 6. Transposing reality.
Project 7. Develop your sense of geometric form.
Project 8. Abstract Expressionism.
Project 9. Poetry illustration.
Project 10. A formalist assignment.
Project 11. A self portrait.
Project 12. A nude.
Project 13. Pastel or oil crayon drawings.
Project 14. Pop art.
Project 15. Op (optical) art.
Project 16. Structural space concept.
Project 17. Collage experiment.
Project 18. Acrylic tests.
Project 19. Oil painting.
Project 20. Watercolor.
Project 21. Apply the "Nautical Anatomy method" to other subjects.
Project 22. Color experiments.
Project 23. A construction based on a two-dimensional painting or drawing.
Project 24. Figurative and Abstract.
Project 25. Found objects and Assemblage.

1

PROJECT 1.
CONTOUR DRAWINGS FROM NATURE

Plants, cityscapes, and landscapes. Try for direct flowing and free outline with thin pen line, marking pens, brush. Explore the use of pencil and dry-brush with added tonal passages over outlines. Keep a sketchbook and draw constantly.

1. Pen contour drawing made rapidly on the spot — a quick notation to capture the character of the architecture along a street in Paris.

2. Dry brush technique. A watercolor brush used almost dry to produce a broken line and tonal effect by scrubbing out ink on a piece of scrap paper before using.

3. A traditional soft pencil technique used on a semi-rough paper with varying pressures to produce light and dark strokes.

2

3

PROJECT 2. PERSPECTIVE USED AND DISMISSED

Read and study about elementary theories of perspective. Search out master drawings of architectural subjects and analyze them —Piranesi, Durer, Guardi. Study Oriental and Byzantine renderings of space. Consult the Cubists and their theories of space projection on a flat surface. Use or dismiss perspective at will but learn what and how to use it, and when to forget its theories. Study the use of reverse perspective, the fracturing of planes, the oriental projection of pictorial space.

PROJECT 3.
DIRECT DRAWINGS FROM NATURE

A straightforward, sensitive rendering of flowers in your garden, or a branch and a shell. Take a morning off and look at the infinite wonders of a rock garden, a park pathway, a sprig of forsythia. Bring the close-up study to bear on it and copy it as well as you can, using contour or outline only.

Try the same thing with volume emphasized, shadows and tones in pencil, wash, or charcoal. Make a page of details from the subject you have chosen. Study the drawings on pages 106-109. Search out some of the fine nature studies of Durer, Da Vinci, Lebrun, and Baskin. Take a look at the watercolors of Demuth, Hokusai, Van Gogh. But look closest of all at the subject *you* are doing and *your* drawing, for this is the one, for this lesson, we are most concerned with.

Wash drawing by Leonard Brooks.

118

Notations from nature.

PROJECT 4. SALVAGING A "DUD"

Somewhere you have a sketch that didn't come off, a painting that should have been a fine one and somehow failed. You feel it has possibilities, could be repainted, redrawn. Now is the time to take it out and give it some calm criticism. Why does it fail? Is it the color, the drawing, the composition? Is it overdone,

overworked? Would it come to life if you changed to another medium and tackled it again? Perhaps by now you have made progress; pictorial space and its problems are a bit clearer to you, negative space also. See what can be done with this material, which you already have and which is only awaiting a fresh chance.

119

PROJECT 5.
A POSTER FOR YOUR EXHIBITION

You have worked hard and long. Your exhibition is ready and you must have a poster for it. It should express you and your work above all. It may be figurative, abstract, or combinations of both. The specifications of printing are:

Size 17 by 27 inches.

Three flat (unshaded or modulated) colors suitable for silk screening.

Use any theme you wish. Adapt a drawing or painting of yours to the design or create a new one. Remember it will be seen everywhere and will serve to represent you. The Brooks poster reproduced here was done in orange-brown, black, and gray on white paper. One thousand copies were printed for this exhibition. The Etrog poster is in tones of yellow and white on dark gray paper.

Poster for an exhibition, by Leonard Brooks.

Poster for an exhibition, by Etrog.

Gallery Moos, Ltd., Toronto

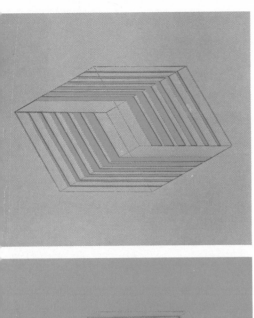

Structural Painting by Rocco Borella. A reverse color scheme using same design motif.

Composizione 15 by Mauro Reggiani. Oil on canvas.

Silent Light by Harold Town. Oil on lucite.

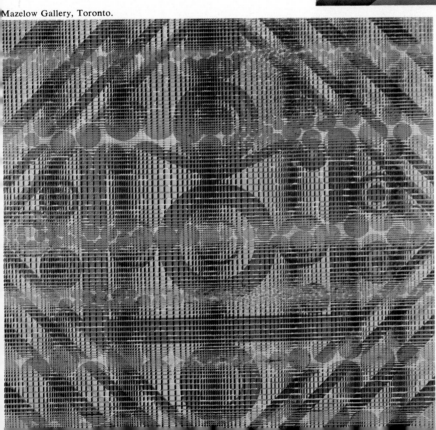

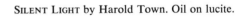

Photograph of shrimp nets.

PROJECT 6. TRANSPOSING REALITY

Here are photographs to examine. What can you do with them to make interesting drawings or paintings? You may wish to change proportions. Make them large or small. Use any medium you wish.

Make an analysis of linear composition.

Study volume and pictorial space possibilities, the essential and dominant forms.

Construct suitable black-and-white interpretations.

Invent color schemes: cold, warm, or a contrasting set of colors.

Change the actuality as you wish, but know *why* you are changing it. "Fracture" the planes, overlap areas distort and emphasize — but do it with reason; do not turn things upside down without meaning. Do not try to "copy" the photographs.

Interpret them, transpose them to your own statement and ideas.

SARA, MARFIL. (Photograph by Reva Brooks.)

122

PROJECT 7. DEVELOP YOUR SENSE OF GEOMETRIC FORMS

A small-mural commission has been offered to you. It must express some of the tension of city life, reflect the movement and feel of city transportation, with direct reference to actual forms of cars, planes, etc. You are confined to using straight lines and diagonals only — no curved lines. The design will be made from your plan using mosaic and inset metal rods for the lines. It is to be ten by three feet. Your sketch is to be done in any size you wish. The mural shown here was done in acrylic by York Wilson.

Mural by York Wilson.

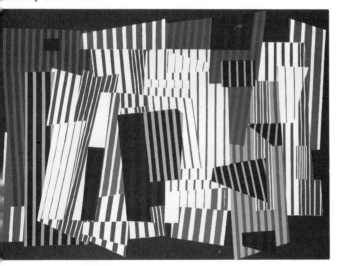

PROJECT 8. ABSTRACT EXPRESSIONISM

You are thinking of your visit to the studio of our artist friend. It was exciting to watch him let loose on that large canvas where no holds were barred and you almost felt the tingle of excitement that flowed through him and into the end of the brush as he worked so quickly and assuredly. Your last few assignments, which demanded so much control and smooth discipline in formalist approach, seemed to lack this passion and emotional release. Austerity may be fine sometimes and for some painters and students, but is it for you? Out with the paint box and the large brushes and the largest canvas you can lay your hands on in your studio. This is going to be one of those free-for-all projects in which anything goes. Perhaps you are thinking of those exciting Klines you saw at the museum, of those de Kooning colors that sang out from the wall in his last exhibition. This way of painting captures the intensity of a feeling and a mood.

Your theme, then, and the start of a lively canvas. What will it be? What has been lurking in the back of your mind that has been demanding expression and the paint brush?

Memories of a person, a place, the sadness of late autumn, gray melting-snow days, the tumble and color of the circus you saw, the flicking of night sounds across the city as darkness settles down? Or have you a mood, a shape, patterns, a clue to begin with . . . a slash of diagonals that throb inside you like music, and must be painted like music?

In blues; all kind of blues, electric and luminous, transparent and thick, dark and light, jagged and smooth. One touch of orange somewhere, or vermilion. Or just a black and gray background acting as a foil for the stark forms on it.

Work any way you want. In oils or acrylic. Forget the rulers, the tapes, the careful considerations of geometrical progression. Let your instinct take over and tell you what stroke must follow what. It's *your* picture and only *you* can feel and know what you want and desire of it.

It must be at least 30 by 36 inches or larger. Big brushes, lots of paint. Stand up to it and engage yourself in the struggle. Begin with all the confidence you can summon up and don't stop until you have finished it — or it has finished you.

Ink drawing by York Wilson for *Hagiwara Poetry,* translated and interpreted by Graeme Wilson. This is one of a set of drawings for the book published by Tuttle, Tokyo, Japan. (Courtesy of the publisher.)

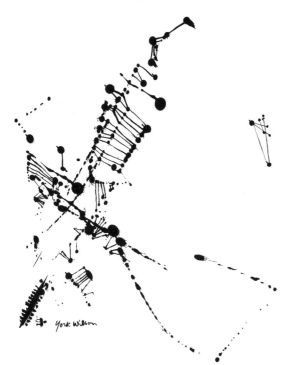

You have a favorite poet. Make a drawing inspired by one of the poems in his *Collected Poems.* Design a book jacket for the volume, in two colors, expressive of his writing. Size of book is 6 by 8½ inches. You *feel* the poems and are impelled to try to *interpret* them, not merely illustrate them. Shown here are a drawing and a book jacket made for publication.

Two-color book jacket for *Collected Poems* by Earle Birney, done in variations of orange and grayed blacks, by the author. (Courtesy McClelland & Stewart.)

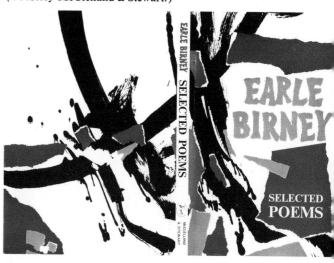

PROJECT 10. A FORMALIST ASSIGNMEN

The morning is clear-cut, fresh; the air shimmers, the sun dances across the garden lighting the trees in a sparkle of green emeralds. A few bright flowers dot the borders of the stone walk. A bird flicks its way through the peach tree, a dark moving spot against the cerulean sky. The world is good this morning. It is a morning to paint, joyously, with the feeling of thankfulness that we are alive and able to enjoy such wonders.

But what to paint? And how to paint it? Our assignment this morning says nothing about green sunfilled gardens. In fact, it says that the canvas is to be an experiment in non-objective picture making, a formalized austere, controlled construction, free from any imitation of nature or visual beginnings. It is to be lesson in formal expression. We are asked to draw from within ourselves, using the limitations of structural and formal means, a composition that will be meaningful, beautifully made, and without literary illusions or subject. Where does our good feeling come in here, our joyousness? Let us see how we can interpret such a feeling in these apparently cold and unsympathetic terms.

Do we want a title or shall we simply use the date, "May 10," to mark the fact that today we painted our picture, a favorite device of contemporary title-making. Fine. Now we have a title, the canvas, the paint. More important still, we have the energy and the desire to do a painting.

Think about it for awhile. May 10, a brilliant day, clear, sharp, colorful. Expressive lines are already suggesting themselves. Let's dig further into our subconscious selves. Take a piece of charcoal, fill some spaces on paper. Try diagonals; try verticals; try horizontals; try curved and rhythmic lines. Let yourself go and see what happens. But remember, this is to be *formal* and directed, no wild emotion here, no action painting. This is a *controlled* exercise — drawing with straight line divisions, geometrically conceived. You are not an impressionist or expressionist painter this morning. Trees and flowers are not your material, though they may have started you off by suggesting certain relationships of line and space.

Look over your scribbles. Try a few more. Do any of them seem to interest you, have a life of their own? Are they worth developing? Such trials will often start the picture on its way, begin the flow of energy that must bring about the picture.

Now the imagination can really go to work. Can you visualize that note finished, painted out fully and carefully? Has its notation anything for you? Does it set up and satisfy some visual reaction worth completing?

If it does, try it now on a 16- by 20-inch canvas. Set out the lines and spacings lightly in charcoal. Fix these with a plastic spray. Mix up four or five batches of color on the palette and begin. The picture is under way. Getting started is half of the battle, and having a direction you wish to go. Now your idea is pinned down; you are on your own and must reach your own conclusions. Put yourself through the experience of painting formally and in a controlled precise manner with close attention to every move. Use an orderly

procedure, block out the large open areas, draw the lines and curves with considered care. Thin out the paint with a good turpentine and a touch of linseed oil. Use a ruler if you wish, and select a sable or bristle brush for the job in hand. Can you add up those spaces, geometric divisions of shape, line, and interval, into a unity that satisfies you?

Your assignment in formalism is over. Perhaps you now realize that this way of working is not your way, but from now on you will have a better idea of what goes on in the mind of the constructivist as he works; you will have had first-hand experience of one way of working in the abstract idiom. Is what you are doing any different from the lay-out man sketching out his linear spacing of text for the daily newspaper? Is it merely a decorative exercise in arranging a few lines? This is what you must answer for yourself, and decide the comparative value of the two. Pin up a Mondrian print on your wall for a few days and see if it satisfies or annoys you. Study the Italian paintings shown on pages 92 and 93.

You will now realize that it is the intention and profundity of impulse that makes the painting a work of art.

Remember the strict disciplines of the early Constructivists who rejected the German Expressionists of the Bauhaus School — men such as Albers, Mondrian, and others who cleared away what has been called the "untidy feelings" (Hilton Kramer) to find an austere and controlled formalism, which left little, if anything, to chance.

TEMPO SETA NUMERO F by Attilio Carreri, 1967. Oil on canvas.

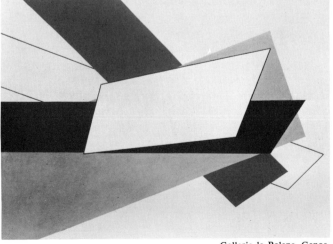

Galleria la Polena, Genoa.

PROJECT 11. A SELF PORTRAIT

Can you really draw — or have you been avoiding it, skipping its problems with plenty of talk about how "basic drawing" is useless? It might be interesting to test yourself here. You may even use the ruler and compass and do something very interesting. The project is to make a self portrait, in any manner or style you wish. Have you seen the portraits by Jacques Villon, the Cubist paintings of his friends with the lines and planes of construction and spatial projection? Or the early geometric Picasso series? Or the portraits by de Kooning, Bacon, Nolan, and Cuevas? Here then is your assignment. Any medium, any technique. We only ask that you are the subject and that when you present your effort it will be recognized as a portrait of you — unmistakably. *You,* portrayed and interpreted in any style or manner. Do you think you can do it?

OLD WOMAN SEATED by Louis Ribak. Ink and wash drawing.

BEATRIZ by Diederich Kortlang. Pastel.

126

PROJECT 12. A NUDE

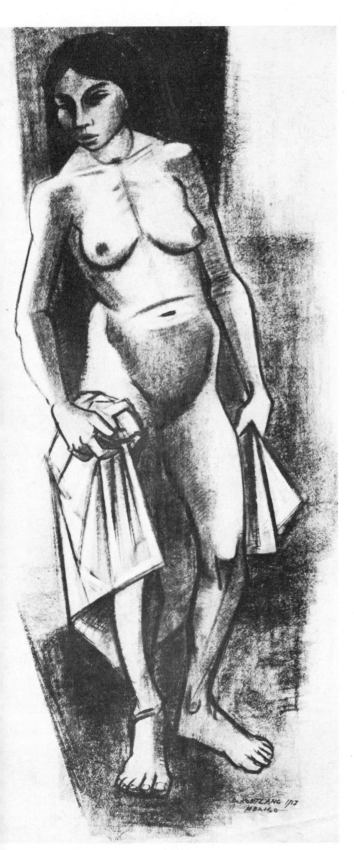

A figure is set in front of you. You are asked to do a set of drawings from the female model. Five minute sketches, catching the gesture, the essential lines of the pose. Forget the anatomy rules, and scribble down as well as you can some of the character of the pose.

If you have no model, only yourself, draw from your mirror image. If your mirror is too small, use a fine photograph of a nude and do the best you can; it is not the same but it is better than nothing. Do the same set of drawings from a male figure and from a child's figure. Use a clothed figure and imagine and see the construction underneath — a transfiguration not too difficult to make with today's revealing fashions. Develop this drawing into an oil painting.

Two Nudes by Matheos Florakis. Oil on canvas.

Standing Nude by Diederich Kortlang. Charcoal and conté.

HARBOR AT RHODES by Leonard Brooks. Collage and acrylic.

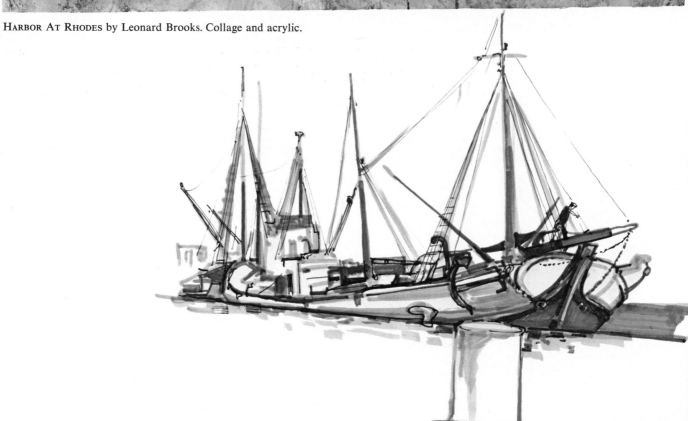

RHODES, GREECE — PAINTINGS AND DRAWINGS

The brilliant orange and white boats, still fashioned in the long sleek lines of vessels from antiquity, the old mills still guarding the port after countless invasions, the dark brooding skies, and the crusaders' fortress — these elements are legitimate and exciting material, a challenge to the painter.

Shown on this page are a group of notes and sketches that preceded the collage-and-acrylic painting opposite. These were research drawings for detail, compositional possibilities, and to feel at home with the subject sufficiently to shift it around from actuality and photographic seeing. The forms have been altered, the mood of the moment emphasized, color and textural changes have been made.

This is one way of working from nature, although the painting was made in the studio later. It was Bonnard who said, ". . . if the object is there while one is working, there is always the danger that the artist may be captivated by the implications of the direct, immediate view, and lose the original ideas as he goes on." (1943)

PROJECT 13.

PASTEL OR OIL CRAYON DRAWINGS

Buy yourself a few selected soft pastel chalks. Try out their colors and texture before assaying a drawing or painting. Choose a subject, perhaps a still life, and work in a small area. Rub, smudge, and apply direct clean touches.

Do the same with a number of oil-pastels, Try diluting them with turpentine to make a wash. Work on dark papers, on velvet surface paper specially prepared for pastel. Draw in pen and ink or brush first, and touch up with these colored crayons. A useful technique for quick sketching out of doors.

Crayon Sketches.

PROJECT 14. POP ART

ard-edged painting of a figurative subject drawn from
ontemporary material . . . no romanticism here! The
nadorned and unpainterly surfaces of bright colors
nd flat color fields. The realistic and pertinent subjects
f our modern life. The impact of clean sharp shapes
nd edges. Try it as an experiment — and look over
e work of some of the well-known practitioners of
is kind of art, in the original if this is possible.

PASSPORT by Elias Dekoulakos. Oil on canvas.

Clean geometrical repeat patterns of a structuralist kind. Fool-the-eye designs that twist and move pictorial space at will — an interesting field of work for the design-conscious painter. Contrast this with the psychedelic approach and observe its near relation to much of the whirling spirals of the art nouveau done at the end of the last century (Aubrey Beardsley and William Morris), later renewed and revived.

OPERA NUMERO F by Gianni Stirone, 1966. Synthetic enamel on canvas. Galleria la Polena, Genoa

PROJECT 16.
STRUCTURAL SPACE CONCEPT

The paintings reproduced on pages 92 and 93 will provide study for your work in the geometric and structural space concept. Other examples are scattered throughout this book and you will soon realize the variety possible with the use of formal means, simple areas, minimal compositional arrangements of line and mass. Try these with shaped canvases and unusual formats as illustrated in the work of the artists reproduced on page 74. Use acrylics, and masking tapes for blocking out areas. Try for clean hard edges and precise fields of color.

PROJECT 17. COLLAGE EXPERIMENT

Use cut up letters, newspapers, and some marble dust to assemble a lively and free vertical panel, as shown - a first exercise in using papers, cut and torn, for collage making. Your experimental collages need not be large, for example, 10 by 4 inches. Use a limited color scheme or work one in black, white, and grays.

Vertical collage.

Bottle collage.

Try a series of exploratory uses of acrylic pigment. Paint in transparent fashion, paint thickly, try using Gel or painting medium; add marble dusts or sand to thick pigment.

Experiment with full saturation of pure color. Try various mixtures. Apply with knife or with brush. Mixed techniques using underdrawings in pen or marking pen, with washes placed transparently over the drawing. Make hard-edged brush strokes as well as strokes with soft broken touches. Try different surfaces — paper, gesso-grounds, rough and smooth. A morning's work will help you master the media if you observe and note the various qualities peculiar to the plastic pigments.

WHITE MORNING MOON by Leonard Brooks. Acrylic on canvas.

Two small oil-on-board panels by Leonard Brooks.

PROJECT 19. OIL PAINTING

Small panels made on the spot from the subject. Large canvases in which you develop your serious themes to their fullest. Try versions of figurative, semi-abstract, and non-objective themes, searching for the particular way that seems to suit you best. Conscious study of technical possibilities open to you. Try thin, thick, combined techniques; palette knife, brush. Read *Oil Painting — Traditional and New* by the author for an understanding of some of the more complex technical ways of working.

PROJECT 20. WATERCOLOR

Use all the knowledges and experiences you have had in the course to do a full-page watercolor. Choose any idiom, realistic or abstract, that appeals to you and carry it through to completion as a serious creative task. Tackle a subject that inspires you and forget all the rules and "isms" in an effort to express something of yourself, your feelings and ideas, in a statement that is freshly alive and compelling. A large order? With luck — and lots of hard work — you may surprise yourself.

A watercolor exercise.

IOUSTON FREEWAY.

Go to the supermarket or your local garage, take a trip o a favorite industrial subject, or spend a day on the roof-top of your apartment. Visit the park where the buses come by, or have a coffee in the basement floor of a department store while you look about you for possible material for your sketchbook notes. Give yourself time to explore the theme you choose, making a conscious search and rendering of facts. Perhaps you do not need drawn reference and notes and your memory is such that it will bring back all that you

require later, but this is most doubtful, unless you have trained yourself to do so.

Whatever you do, do not fasten on your theme until you find something that moves and excites you visually. Then search out the reason why, refining your seeing until the essence of the subject is distilled and emphasized. Strip away the unessential and simplify in the most meaningful manner possible. It is surprising what can be left out to give impact and meaning to what you finally decide to put in.

PROJECT 22. COLOR EXPERIMENTS

PROJECT 23. A CONSTRUCTION BASED

Using marking pens in brilliant colors or the oil crayons now available for artists, make up a page of free-form abstract designs. These should be based on definite elements of design making, that is to say, incorporating either alone or with combinations of repetition of a motif, or dominance of color, or dominance of light and dark areas, or contrast of curved and straight forms and lines, etc.

Make sure the crayons are oil base, not the old-fashioned child's wax crayons. The Japanese color manufacturers have many varieties of strongly-hued color crayons, which are permanent and have full intensity of pigment. Shown on Color Page 61 are some of the marking-pen techniques used in making design motifs, as well as more representational drawings.

Use material such as wires, board, or string. Such an experiment is shown here made by Roy Robel in his exploration of pictorial and dimensional space.

LEAF PATTERN. (Photograph by Roy G. W. Robel.) Tonal interlockings of light and dark patterns formed by leaves and shadows make a wash-like design for the photographer's sensitive eye. Such a close-up scrutiny of natural forms reveals endless subject matter for the making of drawings and paintings.

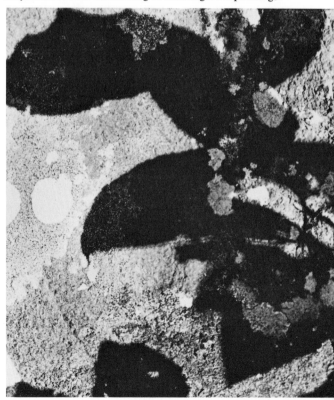

ORM AND SPACE MODULATED by Roy G. W. Robel. 16 by 48
nches. Acrylic on Masonite. Robel states that in this experimental
anel he tried to "modulate form and space." He explains, "I
ried to overcome the 'illusion' of form and space by using the
ctual physical build-up of paint to emphasize the mass of the
ositive areas, and the opposite treatment to push back space in
he negative areas. I employed the reverse side of the
Masonite board to add textural relief."

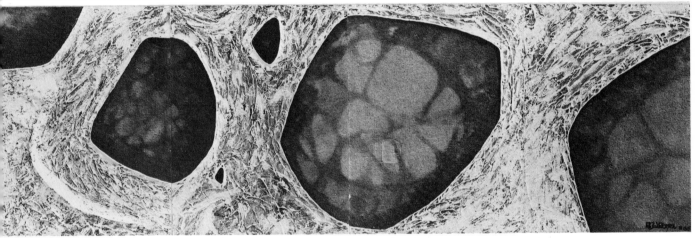

STEEL AND BRONZE PANEL by Roy G. W. Robel. 9¾ by 24½
inches. The painted panel becomes a relief sculpture — "Form
becomes actual and space a real void."

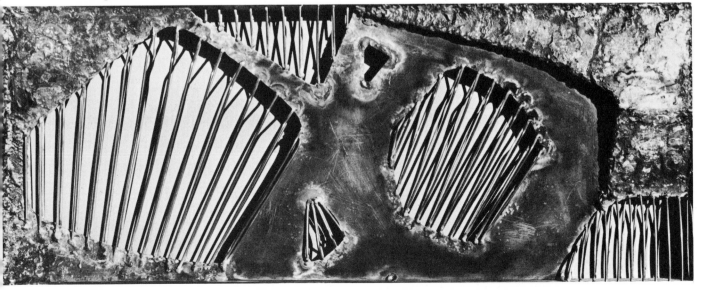

Make two versions of a familiar subject. One figurative and factual in any chosen medium; the other an abstraction using the same subject matter but exploiting fractured planes, emphasis of flat areas, and any other technique to remove it from photographic seeing.

SHRIMP NETS by Leonard Brooks. Large full-sheet semi-abstract drawing.

Abstract wash drawing by Leonard Brooks. Full sheet.

PROJECT 25.
FOUND OBJECTS AND ASSEMBLAGE

Seek out and find objects and natural forms and combine or assemble them in an imaginative presentation — collage, sculpture, or mixed technique.

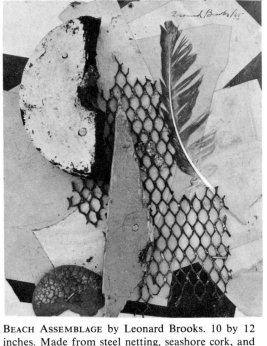

BEACH ASSEMBLAGE by Leonard Brooks. 10 by 12 inches. Made from steel netting, seashore cork, and a feather, mounted on gay yellows and bright reds.

PHANTASMA, assemblage by Sophia Thanopoulou. A bone and eroded brick found along the shores of the Aegean Sea. An imaginative conjunction of disparate elements.

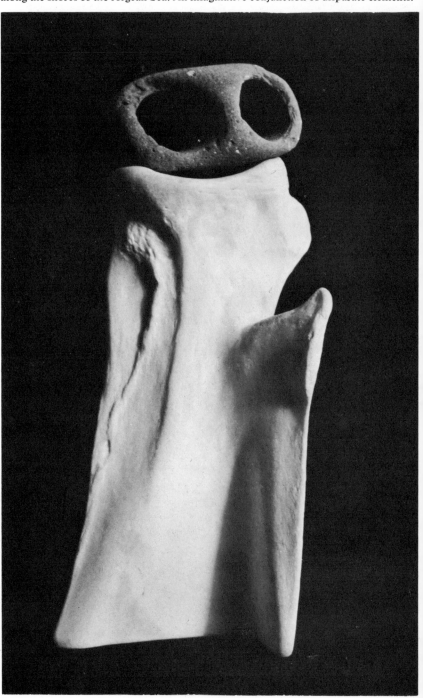

MUSHROOM SPOOR PRINT by Reginald Godden. An abstract design that uses the infinite variety and textures of organic growth from mushroom spoors on blotting paper.   Collection, Leonard Brooks.

Collage by Leonard Brooks. A seashore motif from the Pacific coast. Netting and string with acrylic overpainting assembled into a colorful pattern in yellows and browns. The textures were augmented with marble dust mixed in acrylic emulsion.

NIKI-NIHK by Elias Dekoulakos. Rugged rock forms are grouped into a small assemblage with monumental qualities.

NATURE IMITATING ART. (Photograph by Brett Weston.) A natural composition found and photographed by Weston at Big Sur, California. Here the artist's eye has picked out the detail of an abstract form fashioned by nature and the elements. Textures and rhythmic curved lines form a design that is the prototype of many a painting that uses such non-objective forms expressive of mood and place. Compare this with the large Coastal Collage on page 8, which also takes similar shapes to bear its statement of sea and sky and shore.

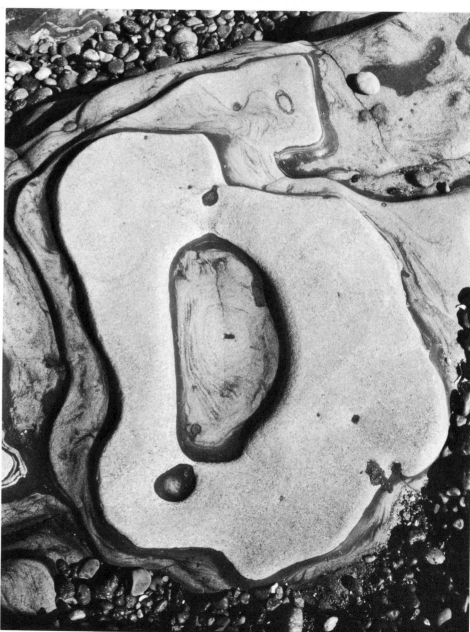

7. TODAY AND TOMORROW

Influences and art of our time, 146

Some thoughts on criticism, 148

What lies ahead?, 149

Influences and art of our times

The constant weighing and assessing of schools and isms in the ever-changing panorama of painting, although of interest and necessary to the art student, can also be an irritant, become a phobia, and too often a waste of energy, which might better be applied to the more practical and decisive problem of producing paintings and drawings. The endless watching of what is the latest style, the countless articles and analytical verbiage produced in art journals and periodicals, the self-conscious anxiety to see that work is ear-marked with the stamp of approval by the critic who happens to be "in" at the moment, the urge to jump onto every bandwagon — all of these can lead to a dispersion of energy and a breathless chase of aesthetic chimeras better left to the dilettante and "talkers" of pictures.

A knowledge of what is being done, and what has been done in the past, a constructive and honest appraisal of what is presented as the best, but always reserving our own judgments — this is another matter. Accepting that the number of artists has become virtually infinite, and the number of paintings along with them, we must, more than ever, learn how to make judgments of our own. We must take from what we see, whether it was done centuries ago or yesterday, and weigh it for ourselves, basing our findings on a background of serious study of many forms and expressions of man's creativity in the fine arts. We must learn to take or reject from all that has gone before, when we need to, as well as accepting only what we want from what today is thrust at us, pounded into us, and, at times, overwhelms us.

Most of the important changes and visual modes that have changed our thinking and shaped what we know as contemporary art today were made in the last seventy-five years or so. (The movements and changing schools of thought beginning from the times of Turner and Constable were examined in some detail in my book *Painting and Understanding Abstract Art:* Reinhold.)

The shaping of influences that moved the artists away from the realistic interpretation of the object, or even to representation of any kind of objectivity, until they produced the purely non-figurative, or non-objective painting, is complex. If we wish to study not only the historical or chronological order, but also to discover how technique and method were revaluated and changed, that is, from the artist's point of view, the research is complicated indeed. New ways and isms overlap, one movement grows into another or puts out tentacles that soon absorb the future experiments and expressions of the new avant-guards. What is considered new and startling becomes old and acceptable. Today, each year brings its classifying and pigeon-holing of each divergent path, or mostly the retreading of well-worn paths by other and new names instead of the original artist-innovators, who were the true creators, new masters, and visionaries.

This turmoil and chaotic recording and savoring of fashion and change is often a healthy thing and is indicative of our mode of life in most civilized parts of the world. It can also be the incessant drumbeat of novelty and superficiality, which has its insidious and harmful side. The calm evaluation, in the midst of upset values, topsy-turvy paeans of praise and heapings of blame for every "new and different" product, is becoming a rare thing. The slow and dignified appraisal has become lost in the rapidity and urgency of getting the message out fast to an eager public anxious to know and hear the latest innovation, conditioned as we are to barrages against the constancy of our beliefs and convictions, whether in buying a box of soap-flakes, a new car, or a painting. We are conditioned to our times, and it is a moot guess whether or not these times are producing for us the art forms we need and deserve, and would have, if we were not so enveloped in those chosen and thrust upon us by the communications media, which dominate much of our daily lives.

To keep track of all these changes and to be aware of what is happening in the world of international art is not the difficult task it once was. Illustrated news magazines devote considerable space to the serious as well as the outrageous aspects of contemporary art. We are deluged with "art forms" — derivative and commercialized back-washes exploited by advertisers and merchants to peddle their wares smartly. The consequent impact and influence on us is formidable.

Drawing by Rocco Borella.

Some thoughts on criticism

In our seminar workshops, one morning a week we bring our work to the studio. Here we have a chance to confront ourselves and the other students in the class with the results of our labors. Watercolors are slipped into mounts, the best drawings are isolated and shown separately from the others, our oils and collages are put on the easel one by one. They no longer belong to us, they are out in the world for all of us to see and to react to. They must stand or fall on their merits. No excuses now and no chance of patching up. Here they are, our creations, and all the verbalizing in the world, all the rationale of our brilliant explanations and discussions will not save us or prove anything beyond the images and symbols we have set down.

As a reader of this book you must imagine yourself in a like situation. You are in the studio, and you are part of the group now revealing whatever progress and understanding you have made, or perhaps, unfortunately, the lack of it.

Learning to assess your own successes and failures is a useful art. A dispassionate evaluation of your work from time to time will be salutary, a time when you consider clearly and without pretensions what lies before you — the exercises, the self-confident pieces, the unfamiliar media you have tried only once or twice, the one you know is the best thing you have ever done and which surprises you even now, when you see it again; its sure sincere quality, its dab of suggestive blue, which is just right, the exciting unusual composition and exuberant brushwork. How did you manage it? Why don't they all come off like that one, especially in the easy and casual manner you worked that magic morning when everything seemed to click and fall into place without a hitch. Why doesn't it happen more often?

This other — the one you fought with for hours and hours — what is the matter with *it*? Why doesn't it come to life like the other painting? It has all the attributes of a good painting; it *should* be good, there's nothing obviously out-of-joint or wrong with it. Then why is it so dull, such a lamentable display of everything that can go wrong with a painting? How little

time has to do with it! "How long did it take you to do that?" you have been asked many times, until you answer, in desperation, "One and three-quarter minutes," or perhaps, "Fourteen and one-half weeks, three hours, and twenty minutes," muttering to yourself, "As if this has anything to do with it."

Self-criticism of a constructive kind can be developed and acquired. Quiet sessions looking at your work: where could it have been improved, what are its good features, its failings? Is it worth trying again or was it a hopeless and confused theme to begin with?

Isolate your best work, hang it on the wall. Glance at it from time to time. Greet it anew when you come into the room. Pretend it isn't there and catch it unaware, sometime, from the corner of your eye, or squint at it from a distance. Confront it suddenly and you may catch a clue to its failure, or why it sends a thrill through you.

It is very easy to become inhibited and hide-bound in your drawing and painting if you are too self-consciously aware of each mark and stroke you are making. It is better to hold such keen, critical sessions away from your actual working projects. Think about what you wish to put down ahead of time, but turn loose on the job in hand without the restrictive inhibitions of a too critical approach. Time enough for this after the work is done.

The professional teacher and critic, trained to his job, knows from experience the difficulties of using the fine critical eye and mind in conjunction to reach his verdict. Right or wrong, his conclusions are based on knowledges and personal observations gained over many years.

When we ask of ourselves impartial and critical assessment of our own work, we must bring to bear the same keen eye and qualities of judgment. Learning how to do this takes practice, but it can be done. With convictions of our own that we feel are valid, construed from experience and knowledge, without prejudices and cynicism, we must organize our thoughts as though we were writing a critical essay about the work.

What lies ahead?

Next door to me, in the old building where I have my Mexican studio (circa 1780), a young Swiss sculptor has his workshop. The other day I came up the antiquated stone stairs to the balcony outside my door and found one of my neighbor's works spread across the ten-foot-wide floor.

Accosting me — there is no other word for it — was a strange assemblage of form and color, glowing in three dimensions on a white platform especially made for its display. Broad orange and black stripes blinked through bent sheets of plexi-glass, corrugated, twisted, cast aluminum curved structures turned and whirled in complex relationship to each other; circular eyes extruded themselves at the end of symbolic arms extending into cavernous tinted spaces; form and design interlocked into a three-dimensional fantasy, which left me rather breathless and wondering.

I found out a few minutes later when the young man knocked on my door and greeted me, explaining that he would like to apologize for taking up all the space on the wide balcony, that there wasn't enough room in his small studio to assemble all the pieces of his last work, and would I mind? He took me into his studio to show me other work in process, pointing out the maquettes for future monumental environments to be set up in gardens and parks of future cities. The structure that had startled me was, of course, only a model. When enlarged to at least twenty or thirty feet high it would be big enough to walk through and around and to really feel the impact of the color and kinetic design that would be incorporated in it.

I studied his tools and equipment — electric cutting saws, drills, casting apparatus — noted the conglomeration of tinted plastic sheets, moulding pastes, luminescent colors glowing from tinted metals. Drawings and sketches in bright colors lined the walls and were piled deep on the floor, sketches I could see interpreted into their solid dimensionality in cut-out partly finished sculptural form. Here was an exciting world of active creativity. The young sculptor told me he was just getting into his stride. What he was really interested in was to combine color, sound, light, and dimension into a new world of visual-audio sensation, which would fuse with the feelings of our modern day. He wanted, he said, to make things that were meaningful, would be used and enjoyed, and that would function as integral experience, not as part of something added on as an afterthought, a decorative piece of cultural symbol. He was beginning to learn how to use the new tools and materials available for sculptors and artists. But it was a slow process, so many of the techniques were new and undeveloped. It was a matter of exploring on one's own all the wonderful possibilities open to a young artist of today, of searching out for oneself fresh concepts, new means and methods, of projecting the excitements of combined and mixed media into new and meaningful experiences.

I thought of the many exhibitions I had seen in Europe and America, where startling objects and sex symbols were becoming common-place, and so much that might have been shocking a few years ago now

GRAPHIC EUROPE by Luc Peire, 1967. 10 by 50 feet. Black paint on white formica.

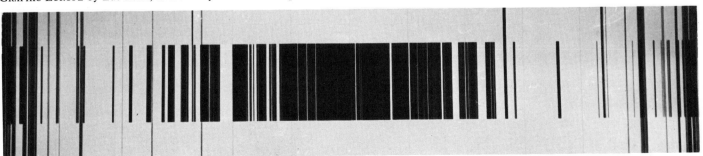

became merely repetitious and at times silly. I thought of the surrealists and the Dadaists who had done so much to free the artist from tradition back in 1911.

I thought of the innovators of new schools and styles of art and how cycles repeat themselves. Was there really nothing new under the sun? I thought of the early primitive sculpture I had seen in Athens — the Cycladic figures done six thousand years ago, which could have come out of Picasso's or Brancusi's studio.

Then I thought again, and knew that today the repetition was *not* the same, for what artist ever had before in this world the atom bomb, the electronic devices, the sounds of microtapes, the lights, fluorescent colors, the wonders of the plastic age to produce miraculous new materials never before found on this earth?

Later that day I came upon these words by Will Grohman, in *Art of Our Time,* ". . . the concept of art has expanded beyond all measure . . . Everything is art, from works in a legitimate tradition to the most daring experiments with light projections or stagily ordered ensembles, and we do not have far to go to the time when mere indications will be given instead of worked-out sketches, incitations for a public, whatever its reactions may be . . . Young people are starting from somewhere else, to some extent the new objects and materials that are forced on them by today's metropolitan consumer world, to some extent the complex structures in which time, motion, light are all involved . . ."

The interest in technical possibilities open to the artist who would deal in sound, light, and color

through electronic developments and modern know-how to which we are all subject in our daily lives — the computer age — has already made its strong mark on many of the younger generation we still call "painters," although they show in "galleries" that are really like laboratories. Open to them is all the wonderful magic of modern technology — the plastics, the involved light and color controls, the stamping and making of objects and assemblages in the new materials of plexi-glass, styrone, etc., which can be moulded and extruded, placed into moving "kinetic" form where nothing remains static but is ever-changing and self-renewing.

Engineers and specialists drawn from the vast and powerful business corporations are eager to have the artists explore for them the design potentialities of their products. We see the results of these researches used in practical ways every day; in the telephone that looks like a piece of sculpture, or, shall we say, sculpture that now imitates the shape of the telephone; in our cars; in architecture and chairs; as well as in the myriad of common utilitarian artifacts thrust at us in advertising pages.

Many artists are working with lights, with plastic sheeting to wrap objects in, assembling old chairs and motorcycle engines in boxes, or just making plexi-glass boxes. Such a repudiation of drawing and painting as we have thought of it for centuries is a legitimate attitude for many young artists. The "tyranny" of the

A large and colorful assemblage of cast aluminum and plastic by Jean Cruchet. Model for an oversize environmental sculpture.

ENVIRONMENT by Luc Peire, 1962. At left, the artist is shown inside his environment. A series of mirror panels reflect his design in endless spatial repetitions to produce an all-enclosing visual sensation of infinite space.
Below, view of the exterior. The "Environment" is enclosed in its box (approximately 8 feet by 11 by 11 feet), which opens to form a seemingly vast room surrounding the onlooker. (Exhibited at the Modern Museum of Art, Paris, and in the Permanent Collection of *Museo de Arte Moderno*, Mexico.)

paint-brush and its rejection from such contemporary studios (which are more like laboratories) is understandable. "Drawing is less and less necessary . . . one thing I wasn't going to do, I wasn't going to draw with the brush," said Stella about his work to Hilton Kramer, during an interview in *The New York Times*.

Recently I have seen art exhibitions where it was necessary to look long and hard before finding a painting that was really a painting, made with paint. The day of the framed picture on the wall seemed to have gone; one looked in vain for just a touch or two of paint on a piece of flat canvas, or a format that didn't bulge, recede, or find itself twisted into toboggan-run channels and roller-coaster curvilinear bulges.

Painting — as painting — may well become a thing of the past before too long. Walls will open up, buttons will press, beams will cross, electrodes will flash, and a whole fantasy of color, form, and electronic "music" will entertain and divert the twenty-first century man from his mechanized existence, relieving him, perhaps, from his boredom as he shoots to the moon or drops in on Venus Station to check on the Satellite Housing he superintends.

One need not be a science writer to envisage this kind of future; much of it is here now. Some of it shows a desperate feeling of urgency to cancel out our old ways of thinking — about the arts, mores, humanities — and everything else of what we have taken in the past for the "solid virtues and truths," by which most of us did and do still live.

Today we can see that art has become a commodity, a status symbol, a good investment, as well as a desperate urge to find something meaningful and

SPACESTRUCTURE by Alexandros N. Tombazis. Greek architect projects a city of the future with prefabricated cellular units integrated into a four-dimensional system using the inventive concepts of the modern designer.

basic to hang on to in the midst of chaotic times of stress and rapid change. Sometimes we can see it become a perverse form of "non-art," non-expression, minimal art, a negation of much that in the past has seemed meaningful and acceptable. But it has also become a need, an honest form of reappraisal of all the values we have taken for granted in the past as truths and virtues, which suddenly have lost much of their meaning for a new generation striving to find itself and to adjust to the sweep of a frightening age of possible nuclear devastation and obliteration.

All of these things — the seriousness and awfulness of matters beyond this book — must need be part of it, for we cannot speak of "creativity," "art," "expression" without these thoughts welling up in our minds and touching our moments of vision and strivings toward a constructive way of existence.

But perhaps we are not all lost or beyond some redemption of a simple, natural approach to our daily round as artists and human beings. Perhaps we still can look to a sky untainted by fallout or the super-jet sound barrier boom. We might, some of us, still want to keep intact some of our cherished ways, even for the few years ahead in which it will be possible for them to exist, even at risk of losing our right to inherit a new and unknown world. We might still paint for joy, and draw with love and pleasure the feelings, forms, and things we know and cherish. We could still, perhaps, draw with love things that exude a healthy and self-renewing splendor in themselves — human beings going about the daily tasks of their lives, growing things and skies — childhood, and joy and sadness — cities, places, water and snow — or even a cat. Or have we really said all that can ever be said about such things? Do we avoid it all and keep ourselves busy making noncommittal and anonymous statements of such non-objectivity and non-subject that we may fear no dread nor doubt within the sure ground of our isolated and self-imposed limitations? Are we going to join the automaton and computer in all seriousness, and try to throw off forever the weakness, the sentiments, the terrible weight of being human and normal and sane? Or are these words, like some of our values and concepts, to be considered inevitably the stupid and primeval labellings of an infantile and misguided lost age not worthy of our mechanized and computer-minded times?

Of course these problems and questions plague you as they do most of us. You need to make a choice of where your sympathies and efforts lie. You are aware, as most of us are, of the deeper manifestations of aesthetic endeavor and these probings will touch home somewhere within you as they do within me. It is impossible to escape them unless you could shut yourself away from any contact with existence today. You may be young enough to accept what goes on about you in a take-it-for-granted style, which has no thought of why life and art are as they are. They "just happened" somehow, and how they came about, what soul-searchings and sweat brought them into being, means little or nothing. Or you may be too tired and too old to care very much about what is happening at the moment or will be happening in the future, living perhaps on former mores and habits.

The chances are, however, that you have thought seriously about these things, and will be thinking more about them as you carry on with your work in *Painter's Workshop*. For drawing and painting, as we have insisted before, is so much more than the mere mechanical act, it is the reflection and expression of ourselves, of our over-all culture and our attitude toward life itself.

I recently examined with great interest the murals at Knossos, and there I found that five thousand years ago artists used the same devices that many artists are using today. Repeat patterns, semi-relief paintings, hard-edge painting, and distortions, they are all there, some of the murals in excellent and wonderful state of preservation. We stood before them marveling how anyone could believe that we are now discovering something new and different.

It is not surprising that Picasso and others have made long and careful studies of the works of Minoan artists. Those free forms along the bottom of the mural — we can almost say that they have some of the feeling of what we like to term "art nouveau," or even of psychedelic art, about them. Wavering lines, spots, rhythmic traceries, and strange color combinations. To see these murals in their actual size and dimension, instead of in reproduction, is worth the trip to Crete.

Today, serious consideration is given to the expressive aesthetic value of such kinds of painting and drawing. In fact, we will observe that many of the artists in international shows who use these abstract modes of approach are applauded and given prizes. "Pure" art, stripped of its romantic figuration, its traditional use of subject, and removed to the highly intellectualized formality of structure, free from all

BLUE LADIES. Wall painting from Knossos, 1600 B.C. (Museum of Heraclion, Crete.)

APE WITH PAPYRUS, ca. 1600-1500 B.C. Wall painting from Knossos. (Museum of Heraclion, Crete.)

illusionistic conventions, is an accepted concept of modern painting. The early small experimental works of such men as Klee and Kandinsky of the Bauhaus, and others, have been blown up into large and overwhelming canvases, which, by their very basic content of stripe, line, or circle, assume a new and at times "non-art" impact that creates a powerful, dehumanized symbolism. This often becomes an echo and a cliché too easily emulated and repeated without understanding, meaning, or deep feeling.

Such rapid changes of approach and stylizations by followers and innovators of schools of painting have their immediate repercussions in the world of fashion and commercial art. We have seen this in the promotion of "Pop," "Op," and other art techniques in a high percentage of newspaper and magazine advertising. Formalized and starkly colored Mondrian dresses had their day, to be eased out by eye-catching geometric patterns that reproduced "optical-illusion" prints to exactitude. Then came the whirl of brilliantly colored "art nouveau" designs, splashing their patterns across fashionable apparel — one more manifestation of our continuing excitement about what is new and different, in every area of contemporary life.

Opposed to this, we see the return of the "figure" movement, seeking to use the object once again as its prime cultural assault. Representation, painting of literal objects, such as coca-cola bottles and hamburgers, or blowing up of comic strip sections to vast size; the use of soup-can labels, crudely painted sex symbols — all of these sign-painter approaches to painting have had a large and entertaining acceptance by American critics, and some of the public. "Pop" art, coming as a shock in 1962 with the work of Lichtenstein, Warhol, Rosenquist, and others, brought a return to figuration in a new, blatant and coarse form. Already this movement has been analyzed, relegated to its supposed place in the serious art history of our times, and has become absorbed in and related to some of the more sophisticated styles of "Op" and hard-edged geometrical painting and minimal art.

Many figurative artists, shunning the hard-edge school, have worked to bring about a kind of combined painting technique that embraces the lessons of the Abstract Expressionists along with those of the more formalized "hard-edge" painters. Thus another kind of painting emerges, less overly-geometric, less wildly expressionist, reminiscent, once again, of some of the early loose paintings of the first neo-Impressionists who sought bold patterns, well-defined linear definition, and brilliant color — a kind of "Fauve" painting closely related to what was done by Vlaminck, Derain, and Matisse somewhere around 1906. So the cycle turns.

THE NINE MUSES by Carlos Mérida.

BIBLIOGRAPHY

BIBLIOGRAPHY

ABSTRACT PAINTING, Michel Seuphor. Harry N. Abrams, Inc., New York, 1962.

THE ANALYSIS OF BEAUTY, William Hogarth; edited by Joseph Burke. Oxford University Press, New York, 1955.

THE ART OF ASSEMBLAGE, William C. Seitz. The Museum of Modern Art, New York, 1961.

THE ART OF COLOR, Johannes Itten, 1961. Van Nostrand Reinhold Company, New York.

ART OF OUR TIME, edited by William Grohmann. Thames and Hudson, London.

THE ART OF PAINTING, 3 Vols. Hawthorne Books, Inc., New York and London.

ART STUDENTS' ANATOMY, Edmond J. Farris. J. B. Lippincott Company, Philadelphia.

ARTISTS AT WORK, Bernard Chaet. Webb Books, Inc., Cambridge, Mass., 1961.

BASIC DESIGN: The Dynamics of Visual Form, Maurice de Sausmarez. Studio Vista. London; Van Nostrand Reinhold Company, New York.

CÉZANNE DRAWINGS, Alfred Neumeyer. A Bittner Art Book, Thomas Yoseloff Inc., New York.

A CONCISE HISTORY OF MODERN PAINTING, Herbert Read. Thames and Hudson, New York.

CREATIVE COLOR, Faber Birren, 1961. Van Nostrand Reinhold Company, New York.

CUBISM AND TWENTIETH-CENTURY ART, Robert Rosenblum. Harry N. Abrams, Inc., New York, 1968.

DESIGN AND EXPRESSION IN THE VISUAL ARTS, John F. A. Taylor. Dover Publications Inc., New York.

DESIGN AND FORM: THE BASIC COURSE AT THE BAUHAUS, Johannes Itten, 1964. Van Nostrand Reinhold Company, New York.

DICTIONARY OF ABSTRACT PAINTING, Michel Seuphor. Tudor Publishing Company, New York.

DICTIONARY OF MODERN PAINTING, Fernand Hazan. Tudor Publishing Company, New York.

DRAWINGS OF THE MASTERS, 10 Vols. Shorewood Publishing Inc., New York.

GEOMETRIC ABSTRACTIONS IN AMERICA, John Gordon. Frederick A. Praeger, New York.

GHIKA PAINTINGS, DRAWINGS, SCULPTURE. Lund Humphries, 12 Bedford Square, London WC1.

HISTORY OF COLOR IN PAINTING, Faber Birren, 1964. Van Nostrand Reinhold Company, New York.

HOW TO USE CREATIVE PERSPECTIVE, Ernest W. Watson, 1955. Van Nostrand Reinhold Company, New York.

THE ILLUSTRATIONS FROM THE WORKS OF ANDREAS VESALIUS. World Publishing Company, Cleveland and New York.

KINETIC ART, Guy Brett. Studio Vista London; Van Nostrand Reinhold Company, New York.

LANDSCAPE INTO ART, Sir Kenneth Clark, London, 1948.

LETTERS OF THE GREAT MASTERS, 2 Vols. Random House, New York.

THE MODERNS, Gaston Diehl. Crown Publishers Inc., New York, 1966.

NICOLAS DE STAËL, Douglas Cooper. W. W. Norton and Company, Inc., New York.

NOTES FOR A YOUNG PAINTER, Prentice-Hall Inc., Englewood, New Jersey.

OIL PAINTING—TRADITIONAL AND NEW, Leonard Brooks, 1959. Van Nostrand Reinhold Company, New York.

THE PAINTER'S SECRET GEOMETRY, A Study of Composition in Art, Charles Bouleau. A Helen Kurt Wolff Book, Harcourt, Brace & World, Inc., 1966.

PAINTING AND REALITY, Etienne Gilson. Meridian Books, Inc., 1957.

PAINTING AND UNDERSTANDING ABSTRACT ART, Leonard Brooks, 1964. Van Nostrand Reinhold Company, New York.

PAINTING IN THE 20TH CENTURY, Werner Haftman. Frederick Praeger, New York, Washington.

PAINTING—SOME BASIC PRINCIPLES, Frederick Gore, 1965. Studio Vista, London; Van Nostrand Reinhold Company, New York.

PAINTING WITH PURPOSE, Morris Davidson. Prentice Hall Inc., Englewood, New Jersey, 1963.

PAINTING WITH SYNTHETIC MEDIA, Russell O. Woody, Jr., 1965. Van Nostrand Reinhold Company, New York.

PATHS OF ABSTRACT ART, Edward B. Henning. Cleveland Museum of Art, Cleveland, Ohio, 1966.

PAUL KLEE, Will Grohmann. Lund Humphries, 1966. London, 1954.

POLYMER PAINTING AND RELATED TECHNIQUES, Russell O. Woody, Jr., 1969. Van Nostrand Reinhold Company, New York.

POST-IMPRESSIONISM, John Rewald. Museum of Modern Art, New York, 1962.

PRACTICAL APPLICATION OF DYNAMIC SYMMETRY, Jay Hambridge. Yale University Press, 1932.

THE PRINCIPLES OF HARMONY AND CONTRAST OF COLORS, M. E. Chevreul; edited and with commentary by Faber Birren, 1967. Van Nostrand Reinhold Company, New York.

THE SHAPE OF CONTENT, Ben Shahn. Vintage Books, New York, 1957.

THE VISUAL EXPERIENCE, Bates Lowry. Harry N. Abrams, Inc., New York, 1961.

WATERCOLOR—A CHALLENGE, Leonard Brooks, 1957. Van Nostrand Reinhold Company, New York.

INDEX

INDEX

Page numbers in **boldface** type indicate illustrations.

Abstract Expressionists, 91, 123, 154
abstractionists, 79, 81, 103-6, 110-1;
   geometric, **23**, 91; Neo-Plastic, 91
acrylic painting technique, 28, **29**, **37**, **66**,
   66-7, **67**, **71**, **74**, **95**, **111**, **112**, 112, 115,
   123, **128**, **129**, 132, 134 *and* Chart (in-
   sert), **134**, **139**, **143**; in collage, 69, 70,
   71, **71**, **128**, **143**; equipment for, 67; in
   monotype prints, 76
action painting, 91, **103**
Albers, Josef, 80, 125
alla prima method, 62-3, **63**, 115
Alpha Color, 53
anatomy, 13, 33, **33**, **35**, 114, 127 *and*
   Chart (insert); nautical, **40**, 41-2, **42**,
   43, **44**, **137**, 137
architectural drawings, 12
art nouveau, 132, 153, 154
assemblage, 115, 142 *and* Chart (insert),
   142, **144**, **151**

Bacon, Francis, 126
bamboo pen, **30**
Baroque style, 27
Baskin, Leonard, 118
batik, **35**
Bauhaus School, 125, 154
Beardsley, Aubrey, 132
Birney, Earle, *Collected Poems,* **124**
Birren, Faber, *Color, Form, and Space,* 80
black and white exercises, 26, 47, **54**, 64,
   79, **101**, 115, 122
Bonnard, Pierre, 22, 32
Borella, Rocco, 91; Drawing, **147**;
   "Structural Painting," **121**; "Struttura e
   colore," **92**
Brancusi, Constantin, 150
Braque, Georges, 17, 32, 47, 62, 79, 114
Breeze, Claude, "Control Center #7: All
   American Boy," **74**
Brooks, Leonard, "Acropolis," **48**;
   "Autumnal," **71**; "Barges Along the
   Seine," **54**; "Beach Assemblage," **142**;
   "Big Sur Waves," **46**; "Cathedral in
   Venice," **110**; "Coastal Theme," **8**;
   collages, **133**, **143**; "Early Morning in
   Sienna," **49**; exercises, **135**, **136**, **141**;
   "First Snow," **19**; "Gondolas," **55**;
   "Grand Canal, Venice, 1961," **49**;
   "Greek Island Harbor," **110**, "Harbor
   at Rhodes," **128**; "Homage to R. L.," **71**;
   "Houston Freeway," **137**; "Knossos,"
   71; "Market Place," **55**; "Mosque at
   Rhodes," **48**; *Oil Painting—Traditional
   and New,* 135; "Paris, 1961," **65**; poster,
   120, **120**; "Quebec," **46**; "Red and Gold
   Collage," **2**; "Rhodes, Greece," **129**;
   "Roof Tops," **54**; "Rooftops and
   Acropolis," **30**; "Rusian Circus," **105**;
   "Sea and Shore," **66**; "Shrimp Nets,"
   140; small collages, **40**; "Sunny
   Market," **19**; "Table-Top," **65**;
   "Table-Top Collage," **110**;
   *Understanding and Painting Abstract
   Art,* 27, 146; "Venetian Canal," **55**;
   wash drawing, **118**; "White Morning
   Moon," **134**; "Wind, Wall, and Sea—
   Hydra," 28, **28**, **29**; "Yellow and
   Black," **96**
Brooks, Reva, **122**
brush drawing, **58-9**, **101**, **106**
brushes, for oils, 63, 123; for acrylics, 66-7
Byzantine tradition, 20, 78, 117

Calder, Alexander, 91
Carreri, Attilio, "Tempo Delta No. 11,"
   112; "Tiempo Seta Numero 2," **93**;
   "Tempo Seta Numero F," **125**
casein, 115
Cézanne, Paul, 17, 32, 33, 114
charcoal, 13, **35**, **64**, 127
chiaroscuro, 78
Cimabue, 78

cityscapes, **58-9**, 59, 115 *and* Chart (insert)
classical style, 27
Cohen, Sheldon, "Arrangement of
   Original Hexagons," **74**
collage, **2**, 24, **40**, 42, **65**, 68-70, **68-70**, 71,
   82, **94**, **96**, **105**, **110**, **111**, 115, **128**, **133**,
   133 *and* Chart (insert), **143**
collage prints, 72, 75, **75**, 115
color, 78-82; in acrylics, 66; analyzed,
   79-81; broken, 78; in collage, 68, 70;
   history of, in painting, 78-9; light as
   basis of, 79; in oil painting, 62-5; relationships, 80; scientific studies of, 80;
   and size, 81-2; watercolor, 56
color experiments, 138 *and* Chart (insert)
composition, 22, 26-9, **26**, **27**, **28**, **29**, 47,
   54, **58-9**, 78, 119
compositional devices, 114 *and Chart
   (insert)*
Constable, John, 78, 146
conté crayons, *see* crayons
constructions, 138-9 *and* Chart (insert), **139**
Constructivists, 91, 125
Corot, J. B. C., 78
Cotman, John Sell, 51
Cox, David, 51
crayons, 115 *and* Chart (insert); conté,
   35, **127**; oil, 130, **130**, 138; wax, 51, **109**
criticism, self-, 115 *and* Chart (insert), 148
Cruchet, Jean, "Assemblage," **151**
Cubists, 17, 20, **23**, 68, 79, 114, 126
Cuevas, José Luis, 126; "Procuress with
   Meat," **37**; "Self Portrait as an Old Man
   with Girls," **99**

Dadaists, 150
Degas, Edgar, **53**
de Kooning, Willem, 56, 123, 126
Dekoulakos, Elias, 103; "Ancient and
   Modern Greek," **37**; "Niki-Nihk," **144**;
   "Passport," **131**
Delaunay, Robert, 79
Demuth, Charles, 118
Derain, André, 154
design, 13, 27, **58-9**, 111, 114, 123, 138,
   149
De Stijl group, 91
Deutch, Peter, "Quadratic," **90**
De Wint, Peter, 51
Dobroruka, Ivan, etching, **26**
drawing, 47, 56, 78, 108, **109**, 114 *and*
   Chart (insert), **116**; figure, 33, 114, 127
   and Chart; language of, 12; techniques,
   14-25
dry brush technique, 116, **116** *and*
   Chart (insert)
Dubuffet, Jean, 56
Dürer, Albrecht, 117, 118

emulsions, 62
enamel, **74**, **93**, **132**
equipment and tools, 115 *and* Chart
   (insert), 149; acrylic, 67; collage, 68-9;
   oil, 38, 62, 103; sketching, 38;
   watercolor, 38, 56
etching, **26**. *See also* graphics
Etrog, poster, 120, **120**
Expressionists, 27, 125
Eyck, Jan van, 62

Fauves, 27, 154
Feininger, Lyonel, 114
figurative or abstract?, 110, **110**, **111**;
   project, 140 *and* Chart (insert), **140-1**
figure drawing, *see* drawing *and* models
Field, Saul, "Hodel's Wedding," **73**
Fisher, Brian, drawing, **100**
Flemish school, 78
Florakis, Matheos, "Girl's Head," **35**;
   "Two Nudes," **127**
Fontaineblue school, 78
form perception, color and, 79
formalist painting, 91, 124-5 *and* Chart
   (insert), **125**
found objects, 115, 142 *and* Chart (insert), **142**
free form, 25

Gandini, Morcolini, "Uguo Modellato
   Dipinto, **92**
Gel, 66, 67, 134
geometric abstractionists, **23**, 91
geometric form, 123 *and* Chart (insert),
   123
George, Thomas, "Norway Series
   III," **101**
gesso, 75, **67**, 134; acrylic, 67; prints, 115
Ghika, Nico, "Rocky Shore," **94**; "White
   Constructions," **88**
glazes, 62, 65, 115
Godden, Reginald, "Mushroom Spoor
   Print," **143**
gouache, 51, 115
graphics, **26**, 47, 72-6, **73**, **74**, **75**, **76**, 115
   and Chart (insert), **143**; drawing and,
   12, 20
Gris, Juan, 114
Grohman, Will, *Art of Our Time,* 150
Guardi, Francesco, 15, 117; "Loggia of a
   Palace," **15**, 18; "Teatro La Fenice,"
   15, 18

Hokusai, 118
Holbein, Hans, 78
Homer, Winslow, 51
horizon line, 15, 17
Hudson River School, 78

imaginative drawing, 114 *and* Chart
   (insert)
impasto, 63, **64**, 65, 67, 115
Impressionists, French, 78, 79
imprimaturas, 62, 63, 115
influences in art, 146
ink, black India, 51; sumi. 53. *See also*
   pen and ink drawing *and* wash drawing
ink resist drawing, **35**
intaglio blocks, wood or linoleum, 72

Japanese tissues, **72**, **73**, *See also* papers

Kandinsky, Vassily, 79, **101**, 154
Klee, Paul, 32, 33, 154
Kline, Franz, 123
knives, *see* palette knife *and* razor blade
Knossos wall paintings, *see* Minoan
   painting
Kortlang, Diedrich, "Beatriz," **126**;
   "Monotype," **76**; "Self Portrait," **35**;
   "Standing Nude," **127**
Kramer, Hilton, 125, 151

landscapes, 115 *and* Chart (insert)
Laville, Joy, "Interior Study," **52**
Lear, Edward, 31
Lebrun, Rico, 118; drawing, **102**
Leonardo da Vinci, 78, 118
Lichtenstein, Roy, 154
light, color and, 79
line, **14**, **23**, 26, **35**, **42-3**, **58-9**, **109**
linseed oil, 67, 115, 125

Mandelman, Beatrice, collage, **82**;
   "Red Time," **94**
marble dust, 66, **111**, 133, 134, **143**
Marin, John, 32
marking pen, **58-9**, 60, **60**, **61**, 115 *and*
   Chart (insert), 134, 138
masking tape, 67, 75, 133
materials, new, for artists' use, 151
Matisse, Pierre, 154
matting, 55
Maxwell, Robert, "Mother and Child," **31**
Mérida, Carlos, "Arquitecturas," **98**;
   "The Astrologer," **95**; "Lil, Cabel, y
   Anabel," **85**, "The Nine Muses," **154**
Minoan painting, 153; "Ape with
   Papyrus," **153**, "Blue Ladies," **153**
Miró, Joan, 56
mixed media, 70, **89**, **94**, **111**, 149
models, 127
Mondrian, Piet, 91, 125, 154
Monet, Claude, 78
monotype prints, 72, 76, **76**, 115

Moralis, Yannis, "The Ultimate Solution," **84, 86-7**
Morris, William, 132
mosaic, 123
Motherwell, Robert, 115

Nash, Paul, 51
nature study, 106, **106, 107, 108, 109**, 114, 116, 118, **118** and Chart (insert), **119**
negative space, see space, negative
Neo-Impressionists, 78, 154
Nolan, 126
nudes, **35**, 127 and Chart (insert), **127**

oil painting technique, basic, 62-5; **19, 63, 64, 65**, 84, **88, 89, 90, 92, 93, 97, 98, 105, 110, 111, 113,** 115 and Chart (insert), **121, 125, 127, 131, 135**; equipment for, 38, 62
Onno, Mai, "Bee," **109**; "Italian Vineyard," **52**
opaque colors, 51
Optical art, 12, 78, 91, 115, 132 and Chart (insert), **132**, 154
Oriental influence in art, 20, 51, 117
Orphism, 79
overpainting, 67, 70, 115

palette knife, use of, 63, **64,** 65, **66,** 67, **111,** 115
paper cut prints, 72
papers, 53, 56, **67, 68,** 69, 75, **85,** 115, 130
pastel, **52,** 53, 115 and Chart (insert), **126,** 130
Peire, Luc, "Environment," **150-1**; "Graphic Europe," **82, 149,**
pen and ink drawing, 13, **23,** 28, **109,** 115 and Chart (insert), 134
pen and wash technique, **15**
pencils and pencil drawings, 13, **58-9,** 73, 75, 114 and Chart (insert), **117**
perspective, 12, 13, 15, 18, **23;** elementary, 15-20, 115 and Chart (insert); dismissal of, 12, 15, 20, **21,** 117 and Chart; isometric, **20**
photographs, **28,** 122 and Chart (insert), **122, 138, 144**
Picasso, Pablo, 56, 79, 126, 150, 153
pictorial space, see space
picture plane, 15, 17, 26, 114 and Chart (insert)
Piranesi, Giovanni Battista, 117
Pisanelle, 56
planes, 122; inclined ("tipped up") 17, 20, **20;** overlapping, 110
poetry illustration, 124 and Chart (insert), **124**
Pointillist school, 78
Pollock, Jackson, 56
Pop art, 131 and Chart (insert), **131,** 154
portraits, 12. See also self portraits
Posner, Myra, "Juggler," **35**
posters, 120 and Chart (insert), **120**
Post-Impressionists, 79
Pre-Raphaelites, 78
prints, see graphics
projects, 115, 116-44 and Chart (insert)
Proust, Marcel, 80
psychedelic art, 153

Rada, Zdenek, "Night of Iguanas," **89;** "Sun," **94**
Ravenna mosaics, 78
razor blade, use of, in watercolor painting, 51, 53, 115; in acrylic painting, 67
Read, Herbert, 104
Reggiani, Mauro, "Composizione Numero 10," **92;** "Composizione 15," **121**
Rembrandt, 31, 56, 78
Renaissance style, 27
Ribak, Louis, "Old Woman Seated," **126;** "Study," **90;** "White Canyon," **94**
Robel, Roy G. W., 139; "Form and Space Modulated," **139;** "Leaf Pattern," **138;** steel and bronze panel, **139**

Rojo, Vincenté, "Abstraction," **98**
Rosenquist, James, 154
rubbings, textural, 72-3, **72,** 115

salt, use of, in watercolor painting, 51
sand, 66
Sargent, John Singer, 53
schedule of projects, 115, 116-44 and Chart (insert)
Schwitters, Kurt, 115
sculpture, 149, 150
scrumbling, 65, 115
self portraits, 126
semi-abstraction, 110
Seurat, Georges, 78
Sisley, Alfred, 78
size, element of, in painting, 81-2
sketchbook-box, 38, **38,** 41, 53
sketching, 31-2, **34,** 130; equipment for, 38; hazards, 36; techniques of, 32-3
Smith, Gordon, silk screen print, **74**
space, negative, 22, 24, **24,** 114 and Chart (insert), 119; pictorial, 17, 22, 26, 117, 119, 122
spatial projection, 20, **21,** 22
spatial relationships, **23**
speedball pen, **25**
Spyropoulos, Yannis, "Intention A," **89;** "Intention B," **84**
Staël, Nicholas de, "Houses at Argenteuil," **105**
Stansfield, Herbert, **108**
starting technique, 103-4, 123, 125
Stella, Joseph, 151
Stirone, Gianni, "Opera Numero 13," **93;** "Opera Numero F," **132**
structural space concept, 133 and Chart (insert)
structuralists, geometric, 12, 91, **92, 93**
Surrealists, 150
Sutherland, Graham, 51
synthetic media, 62, **93**
Synthetic Media and Polymer Painting (Russell O. Woody), 67

Takal, Peter, "Fishes," **109;** "Kneeling Nude," **35;** "Poppies," **107**
Tate, Sylvia, drawing, **109**
techniques, basic, 47-76
tempera, underpainting in, 62
Thanopoulou, Sophia, "Phantasma," **142**
Titian, 78
Tombazis, Alexandros N., "Spacestructure," **152**
tone, **35,** 47, 78, **116**
Tousignant, Claude, "Target," **74**
Town, Harold, "Enigma," **100;** "Silent Light," **121;** "Smoke Grill," **97**
trends in modern art, 149-54
Turner, J. M. W., 31, 32, 51, 56, 78, 146
turpentine, 63, **64,** 66, 67, 76, 115, 125, 130

Van Gogh, Vincent, 51, 78-9, 118
vanishing points, see perspective
Venetian school, 78
Veronese, 78
Villon, Jacques, 126
Vlaminck, Maurice, 154

Warhol, Andy, 154
wash drawing technique, 13, **31, 42-3,** 46, 47, **48, 50,** 51, **54, 57, 59, 109,** 115 and Chart (insert), **118, 126, 141**
watercolor, 13, 28, 47-57, **48, 52, 54, 55, 57, 99,** 115, 136 and Chart (insert), **136;** equipment for, 38, 56
wax crayon, see crayons
Weakland, Anna Wu, "Birds in the Rain," **106**
Weston, Brett, "Nature Imitating Art," **144**
white watercolor, 51
Wilson, Graeme, Hagiwara Poetry, **124**
Wilson, York, 123, **123, 124;** "Kabuki," **112**
wood engraving, see graphics

Zappettini, Gianfranco, "Struttura en BX 5," **93**

751
B
BROOKS, LEONARD
Painter's workshop

13624

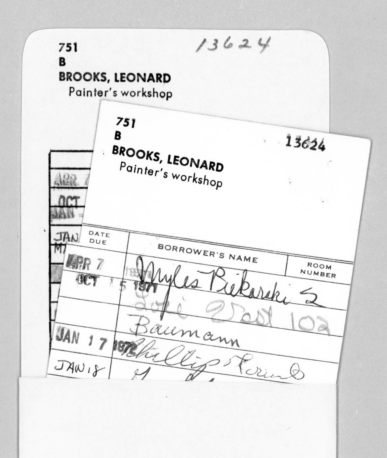

751
B
BROOKS, LEONARD
Painter's workshop

13624

DATE DUE	BORROWER'S NAME	ROOM NUMBER
APR 7	Myles Bekarski	2
OCT 15 1971	*West*	102
	Baumann	
JAN 17 1972	Phillip Krind	
JAN 18		